W9-CGQ-713

THE ASTROLOGY OF LOVE & SEX

THE ASTROLOGY OF
LOVE & SEX

A MODERN COMPATIBILITY GUIDE

by Annabel Gat
Illustrations by Jess Rotter

CHRONICLE BOOKS
SAN FRANCISCO

To Zita Body Slonevsky and
Megan Spencer King—
my love affair with astrology is thanks to you two!

Text copyright © 2019 by Annabel Gat.
Illustrations copyright © 2019 by Jess Rotter.
All rights reserved. No part of this book may be reproduced in any
form without written permission from the publisher.

Library of Congress Cataloging-in-Publication Data:

Names: Gat, Annabel, author. | Rotter, Jessica, illustrator.
Title: The Astrology of Love & Sex: A Modern Compatibility Guide /
by Annabel Gat ; illustrated by Jessica Rotter.
Other titles: Astrology of love and sex
Description: San Francisco, CA : Chronicle Books LLC, [2019]
Identifiers: LCCN 2018047448 | ISBN 9781452173436 (hc : alk. paper)
Subjects: LCSH: Astrology. | Love—Miscellanea. | Mate
selection—Miscellanea. | Interpersonal relations—Miscellanea. |
Astrology and sex.
Classification: LCC BF1729.L6 G38 2019 | DDC 128/.46—dc23 LC
record available at https://lccn.loc.gov/2018047448

Manufactured in China.

Design by Sara Schneider.

10 9 8 7 6

Chronicle Books LLC
680 Second Street
San Francisco, CA 94107
www.chroniclebooks.com

Contents

Introduction

When I ask people how they got into astrology, the answer I hear most frequently is: "I found the occult section at the bookstore, or library, and I never left." Heading to the bookstore to read astrology books with my friends, or going on a solo mission between whatever mundane school or work responsibilities I had, was a favorite activity of mine as a young astrologer—especially reading the compatibility books. Many of us are attracted to astrology because we want to better understand ourselves and the people in our lives, and the archetypes expressed by the signs of the zodiac serve as a fantastic vehicle for doing just that.

Astrology is an ancient study, but it is also a symbolic language that evolves as we as a society change. Today, sexuality and gender are no longer rigid and finite concepts. Society's understanding of gender roles, identity, and sexuality are evolving, and there's a wide array of experiences and perspectives that can't be contained by the old astrology books of "Aries Man, Pisces Woman." While writing this book, I reflected on my work as an astrologer with people of varied backgrounds, sexualities, and gender identities as well as monogamous and polyamorous relationships to explore how each zodiac sign approaches love and dating.

Things today are different on a technological level, too—we are no longer waiting at home for our telephone to ring (could you imagine?). Now we are trying to avoid being "ghosted" by people we can follow (and be continually reminded of) on social media, or being bombarded with information about what our crush is eating for lunch. Falling in love on an app is no longer unusual; neither is being dumped via text. These are typical aspects of modern dating that last century's astrologers could never have imagined: as time changes, the way we write about astrology and compatibility changes.

In this book, you will find profiles for each of the twelve zodiac signs, outlining their vibe: their strengths and weaknesses, turn-ons and turn-offs, and so on. You will also find sections devoted to compatibility between each of the zodiac signs, detailing the ins and outs of the partnership. Each chapter was written with the many stories I have heard over the years in mind, as well as with astrological know-how, which you can read more about in the section "How Does Compatibility Work?" There is also a quiz that, should you be looking for love and wondering whom to hook up with next, you can take to see which sign in the zodiac might be well suited for you at that time.

what is ASTROLOGY?

People often ask me if astrology is a science, or if I "believe" in astrology—what is this ancient, yet New Age subject? In the past, yes, astrology was regarded as a science, but we have outgrown our need for the stars to function in this way. Do I "believe" in astrology? No, I do not "believe" in astrology. I use it as a tool. It is a language for understanding ourselves and our circumstances. I am totally comfortable with using something as a tool without "believing" in it. I do not need something to be true or a science for it to be valuable for me—for example, art. I like art! You probably do, too. And, in the instances that I use astrology for divination, I am capable of suspending my logical mind for a few minutes of whimsy, for the sake of thinking about things in a different way.

I do not believe in astrology, but I do trust it, or rather, I trust the conclusions I have come to about myself—which do change over time, of course—that have developed through my study of it. All this to say, you do not need to "believe" in astrology or flush logic down the toilet to get something out of this book. I promise. Just as we need a compatibility book for the twenty-first century, we also need to leave behind the notion that you cannot be a scientific person while enter-taining symbolic concepts. Do you like art? Books? Movies? Is music real to you? Then astrology can be, too. It does not matter that it is not a science that can be replicated in a lab.

LET'S TALK QUICKLY ABOUT SOME MISCONCEPTIONS

Has your zodiac sign changed? No. A misconception circulates every once in a while that due to the precession of the equinox, the whole zodiac wheel is screwed up and everyone is a different sign now. But no, your sign has not changed. Your zodiac sign is based on the seasons as experienced here on Earth. The zodiac wheel opens with Aries, signifying the spring equinox (at least, in the northern hemisphere!), and ends with Pisces, after the Sun leaves its time at the end of winter. There are four seasons, each containing three signs—leaving no room for Ophiuchus, sadly, so the rumored thirteenth sign doesn't have a place in this book or any impact on how compatibility is explored in these pages.

Also, cusps: they are not a thing. The Sun is either in one sign or in another. That's how it works. The zodiac wheel is 360 degrees, with each of the twelve signs covering 30 degrees of the wheel. The Sun is located in either one degree or another. I will *gladly* accept anyone telling me they think they are a sign that they were not born under because they simply want to be that sign, but I will always roll my eyes at someone who tells me they are born on a "cusp."

So, what *is* a thing? Getting lured in by the beautiful books on astrology at the bookstore—we all seem to have been there. Being drawn to the magic these books contain and taking a break from the everyday world to reflect on life and love with the stars, the planets, and the zodiac. Sitting with friends and reading from our favorite astrology books about our crushes is seriously some of the most fun I have had learning astrology, and more importantly, learning about myself. I hope you enjoy it, too!

how does COMPATIBILITY WORK?

Astrology is a very deep subject, and because I know you're lovesick and want to cut to the chase, we'll keep this brief: there are twelve signs on the zodiac wheel, and the distance between two signs speaks to the kind of lessons that couple will experience.

The sign before you on the wheel teaches you to trust your intuition and to explore your shadow side, while the sign ahead of you teaches you about self-worth and security. The sign two ahead of yours teaches you all about communication, while you teach the sign two signs back about friendship and community (although as we teach lessons, we learn them, too!). The sign three signs ahead teaches you about building a home, and the sign three signs before yours teaches you about building an empire. Creativity and celebration are lessons learned with the sign four places ahead, and the sign four behind encourages you to break free of your limitations and explore the world. The sign five signs ahead teaches you how to develop healthier habits, and the sign five signs before yours teaches deep lessons about intimacy and sharing, both emotionally and materially—these relationships push both parties to adjust in order to make things work. The opposite sign on the wheel, six places away, teaches us to compromise—opposites certainly attract, and they have a lot to learn from each other, as do couples who have the same zodiac sign and learn from each other's successes and mistakes.

You'll learn more about these concepts as you read the compatibility section of each chapter.

Examining these relationships between the signs relative to each other on the zodiac wheel was part of the process I took to write this book. The other part? Speaking with my friends, lovers, students, and teachers of different backgrounds, gender identities, sexualities, and relationship types. Astrology is a tool, and it is also a language. An astrologer who doesn't *practice* this language by talking with others can't possibly speak to compatibility, no matter how many theoretical texts they read on the subject. I spent years learning about others' experiences, which was a crucial part of writing this book. On that note, I want to remind you: anything you read in any astrology book is just a theory—until you test it out and find out for yourself. Your lived experience will teach you everything you need to know about compatibility—this book is just a fun (and smart!) starting place!

Have you heard that you're most compatible with people whose signs are the same element as you? Or that you should never date a certain sign? These ideas aren't entertained in this book. I hope that you'll never read some other compatibility book, or some write-up online, that screams, "Incompatible!," leaving you deflated and hopeless—ignore them! A *person* wrote that, not the creator of the heavens.

You are *not* your Sun sign. You're a person; the person you are dating is also a person. People can choose to work through their issues, so believe me, any two signs can get along if they want to. There is no "star" rating in this book for signs, summing up how well two signs will get along.

If you visit a competent, qualified astrologer with copies of your and your love's birth charts (with your lover's consent, of course), the astrologer would read that information in more complex ways than any Sun sign compatibility book could give you. This book is a first step to understanding astrological compatibility—it's a fine last step, too, but don't confuse this book for being all that astrology has to offer. An astrologer would consider many other planetary placements, the angles between the planets, and the houses, and would combine your charts in different ways to examine the energy of the relationship. Indeed, compatibility is far more complex than just Sun signs, but it's a fun place to start, and we may not want to rush to an astrologer with each crush we encounter!

Also, a quick note about Sun signs. The dates for the signs listed in this book are based on estimations; the days may vary based on what time and place you were born. And, yes, find your sign in this book and read all about it. But, also check out your ascendant, also called the rising sign, which speaks to the face you show the world, as well as your Moon sign, because the Moon describes what makes us feel safe and secure. Read for your Venus sign, too, just for good measure, as Venus rules love, beauty, and what we value. Oh, and look at your Mars sign, as Mars is a passionate planet that describes how we chase our desires. In fact, you can read the whole book, because each sign is contained in your birth chart somewhere! Not sure how to find out what your ascendant is, or what the other planets in your birth chart are? There are many online resources that can quickly help you sort this out, using your birthday (including the time and place).

Any sign can be a top or bottom, dominant or submissive, vanilla or kinky, and in this book, we'll explore some of the endless ways the signs like to love, flirt, and fuck based on their energies (there are as many ways to enjoy sex as there are people!). But the best way to know what you're into is to explore (perhaps this book will give you some ideas!), or to ask your lover what they're into. This book isn't the be-all and end-all for what turns the signs on and off: honest communication is the only thing that can get you the answers you are looking for if you want to please your mate!

ABOUT CONSENT

All of the recommendations in this book, from sending nudes, to pursuing a sign that may enjoy being "chased," to kinkier activities, should be done with people who have given you their enthusiastic consent. How do you know whether consent is enthusiastic? A sober, mutual, continuous yes is needed. And how do you know when it's not enthusiastic? Well, if you have to ask more than once, or if you find you're trying to per-suade someone to try something, then there you go: It's not enthusiastic consent, it's pressure, and it's predatory behavior. Also, people have the right to change their mind at any time. A yes to one act doesn't mean yes to all other acts, and certainly doesn't mean someone needs to keep doing an act longer than they would like to, or that they need to do it again if they decide it's not for them.

So, there it is: a summary of how compatibility is approached in this book. I hope you will have hours of fun reading it with your friends and lovers, and I hope, too, that you will close it with a deeper understanding about yourself and the people you care about—not because of the meta-physical power of astrology, but because it's through story-telling that we often make the most profound realizations about our lives. Now, jump ahead to the chapter that's about you and your crush, or take the quiz if you're looking for some inspiration about which sign to flirt with next!

which SIGN should you DATE?

Meander through the zodiac with this quiz to figure out which sign you should set your sights on. This isn't a "one time only" quiz—your needs and tastes will change over time, so feel free to take it again and again.

let's get STARTED!

You believe in love at first sight. You need a partner who is able to live in the moment, and who is spontaneous and brave—you two are ready to dive into love headfirst without looking both ways. Fireworks explode when you two are in bed, yet the postcoital cuddles have an innocent sweetness about them.

Yes: We have a winner! Aries likes things done quickly, whether that's falling in love or being the immediate choice on a quiz! Turn to page 21.

No: Hmm, maybe we should take things slower.

A warm fire is crackling before you; your lover places a mug of hot chocolate with homemade marshmallows in your hand—you feel so safe and cozy with your partner! Not only do you two laugh together all the time, but you're also able to comfortably cry around each other. A handmade quilt wraps you two as you gaze at the stars, after deeply passionate lovemaking.

Yes: Dreamy! I'm so there for moonlit evenings with Cancer. Turn to page 87.

No: You lost me at crying.

Verbal affirmations of love and affection are important to you, so getting a good morning and good night call from your lover always makes you feel cared for. The intellectual connection between you two is spectacular, and physically, your lover's kisses are electric and you're so excited to finally meet some-one who is up for anything in bed.

Yes: Please give my number to a Gemini. Turn to page 65.

No: I don't need a flood of notifications popping up on my phone all day; I'll pass.

When they invited you out for a picnic, you didn't realize that it would be at a graveyard. They have vials of liquids you can't identify hidden away in a secret box under their bed, but it doesn't bother you too much because you're inspired by their ambition, creativity, and ability to be so emotionally present with you. The sex is powerful and intense—to the point of being a spiritual experience.

Yes: It sounds like the stars have aligned for a Scorpio! Turn to page 175.

No: This sounds intense; no graveyard picnics for me, please.

You and your lover are VIPs at all the most important parties, and people always comment on what a photogenic couple you are. You two live in luxury—and treat each other like roy-alty. You inspire each other creatively, and the sex (on silk sheets, and in a king-size bed) is intense and passionate!

Yes: Book us a couple's salon appointment—Leo and I have a big event to go to! Turn to page 109.

No: No thank you, I value my private life.

After a long, whimsical evening of passionate lovemaking and deep, emotional sharing, you two wake up and enjoy breakfast in bed, spending some time interpreting your dreams and talking about your past lives. You're not in a rush to go anywhere—except maybe to the beach.

Yes: I always knew I'd end up with a Pisces—I am psychic, you know. Turn to page 265.

No: This book is great and all, but I don't want to talk about astrology all day with my partner.

You always knew you would end up in a power couple. You're so glad you've finally met someone as career driven and focused as you are! But, equally as important, someone who is up for hot, raunchy sex. You two probably have a room exclusively for sex in your home. Oh, and your partner gives excellent massages.

Yes: Pencil me in with Capricorn! Turn to page 221.

No: I don't even know what I will be doing next month— I can't keep up with a Capricorn's five-year plan.

You've been looking for a partner who really wants a relationship, and the one that you found is unbelievably stylish, intelligent, and popular—your social calendars are always full! You two can talk about anything for hours, from politics to art to sex—and indeed, the mental connection in bed is phenomenal!

Yes: I'm ready for my equal: I'll go out with Libra! Turn to page 153.

No: I don't want to be responsible for deciding what we will be eating for dinner each night.

You need to be attracted to someone's mind, and your partner is a total genius. Plus, they're not afraid to stand out, which you find to be a major turn-on. They're always up for an adventure. You hate being bored, and so do they. They're innovative and love to experiment—in life and in the bedroom!

Yes: I need someone who is intrigued by my unique personality, not intimidated! I'll date Aquarius. Turn to page 243.

No: I've tried enough "new things" for now; who else is out there for me?

You and your partner's perfect day includes: plenty of eating, going to an art show or seeing a concert, and of course, plenty of naps (in big, fluffy beds—being cozy is important to you two!). "Solid" and "dependable" are words that turn you on, not off, and meeting a lover who is slow and sensual in bed is just what you've been craving.

Yes: I want to cuddle with a Taurus! Turn to page 43.

No: I need physical activity or else I get stir-crazy.

You probably met your lover at the library, in the philosophy section. Or maybe it was at a big party—you two love to celebrate as much as you love to study. The sex is fiery and passionate, and probably will eventually happen on a plane because you two love to travel so much.

Yes: I'll need to renew my passport, because I'm so ready to fly to Sagittarius land. Turn to page 199.

No: Vacations are great, but I need a partner who I know will stick around for the everyday tasks and routines life requires.

The tarot card associated with your lover, according to occultists, is the Hermit, but despite this, you never question that your partner is there for you! You love their practical, no-bullshit approach to life. Your first kiss was by a waterfall and you could swear that the animals cheered you two on, like you were in a fairy tale. They're sensual, and are so, so willing to please you.

Yes: I'm very picky, so Virgo is the one for me! Turn to page 131.

No: Hmm, maybe I should take a hint from the sign ruled by the Hermit tarot card, and spend some time alone, reconnecting with myself and my inner truth for a while. I'll take this quiz again later!

ARIES

THE RAM

DATES: MARCH 20–APRIL 20

PLANETARY RULER: MARS
ELEMENT: FIRE
MODALITY: CARDINAL

PERSONALITY

Whoosh—the mesmerizing sound of a flame bursting forth from a match . . . fire is born. Aries, the first sign of the zodiac wheel and a Fire sign, has fought and achieved a miracle: birth. After this success, what's next? Aries is excited to know. They've achieved that difficult step, so surely they can do anything. Passionate and eager, Aries is ready to take charge of everything life has to offer them.

Aries is used to being in first place. They are the first cardinal sign, marking them at the beginning of the season—and in this case, the first season is spring. This distinct place on the wheel makes the Ram an enigmatic force and a strong, independent leader.

Ruled by the planet Mars, they have a strong, independent nature, and figuring out who *they are* is the ram's mission. They are constantly learning how to put their strength, leadership, and ability to fight to productive use. But being independent doesn't mean being alone.

AT THEIR BEST

Energetic and fearless, Aries is a pioneer and a leader who takes no one's bullshit. They have incredible willpower and are inspiring to be around. They're optimistic, but they don't just sit back and assume things will get done—this is a sign who makes things happen. A loyal friend, they've got a big heart and are immensely generous. They're not only one of the most fun people, but they're also one of the most steadfast. They're the ones to take you seriously when you're sad and eager to lend a sympathetic ear. Always a fighter, Aries is consistently willing to go to battle on your behalf and combat whatever is bringing you down. Driven and focused, they find a way to make their failures successes, and they stay fixed on their goals, head butting any obstacles that get in the way.

AT THEIR WORST

Aries has a fiery temper—but don't tell them that, they may blow up. Sometimes arrogant and confrontational, they have a tendency to pick fights when they are bored or haven't had enough physical activity (or sex). Being the first sign makes them a little naïve, and because they are blessed with beginner's luck, they tend to act foolishly and impatiently. They have a hard time slowing down, and it takes a lot of falls before they learn to look before they leap. When working with a group or on a team, they take control without any prompting, but then pout that no one appreciates or understands them when asked to step down from being the self-appointed boss. They find it absolutely incredulous that someone would dislike them—clearly, they are amazing and there *must* be some misunderstanding. Indeed, Aries always knows best. They may be the infant of the zodiac (but they weren't born yesterday, you know), and it's their way or the highway.

LOVE PERSONALITY

Aries can have a short attention span; however, their deep need for love, as well as their loyal nature, outweighs most of their flighty behavior once they meet someone who wins their heart. Indeed, *winning* is a theme in Aries's life. Don't be confused. They're not competitive because they want to triumph over other people—honestly, they hardly notice that anyone else is around as they ram their way through obstacles. They win for themself and on behalf of those they love. Aries is all about *overcoming* whatever trial has been set before them. Aries is the champion of the underdog—and they'll fight for love, even if all the odds are against them. And they deeply want to be with someone who *believes* in them. Aries isn't looking for a "worthy opponent" in love (although they do really enjoy playful wrestling with their lovers!), but one whose strength they admire, who will fight for them as hard as they fight for those they care about.

FIRST IMPRESSIONS

Your first impression of Aries really depends on whether or not you were, somehow, in their way when you met them. Did they crash into you as they were dashing to the bathroom at a party? Did you interrupt their stride as they were on their way to an important meeting? If so, you likely met bossy, fearless Aries: a touch angry and in a rush, they probably blew right past you. There is, of course, another side to Aries (still probably in a rush, ready to pick a fight), who is also genuinely excited to meet you, eager to have a good time (a game of truth or dare is likely, if you meet at a party), and totally magnetic. Aries is a fearless person. Although they should not be messed with, they are extremely fun loving.

They're probably wearing red, driving a sports car, or sporting a bold hairstyle. Unafraid to make a statement, their clothes are often over the top, but sometimes they can surprise you in something totally casual, perhaps even some sportswear thrown in, even in circumstances that might call for something more formal. No one can tell Aries what to do—and that's likely the first impression they'll leave you with!

FLIRTING TECHNIQUES

Aries is spontaneous and impulsive, and they'll likely give you their number before you even have a chance to ask for it. If you meet an Aries online, don't delay meeting them in person for too long, or they'll move on to someone else quickly.

Aries loves making the first move—in fact, if you're too forward, too quickly, it's likely you'll lose their interest. Being pursued too obviously at first makes them feel uncomfortable, but once a rapport has been established, feed their desire for passion and excitement by boldly stating how hot they are. That said, simply asking how their day went also goes a long way with Aries—being genuinely interested in them makes them feel mushy, romantic, and cared for.

Once you two are a little more cozy and affectionate, you can flirt with your Aries by giving them a nice head rub while you watch a movie—Aries rules the head, and nothing gets them drooling like a scalp massage.

DATING STYLE

Let Aries plan the date—unless they tell you they long for someone else to do the planning (and they will tell you very straightforwardly if that's what they want).

Aries, a pioneer, is always discovering new things and finding something to be excited about—and they want to share these experiences with the people they care about, so expect to be given a tour of the places Aries is inspired by and interested in on your date. If it's your turn to plan the date, keep it flexible in case spontaneous Aries comes up with something in the middle of your outing (very likely!).

Aries usually has a great time on group dates, so long as they know they will have quality one-on-one time with you, too. A barbecue with friends on a sunny day, wrapped in their lover's arms—they're into public displays of affection (PDA)—laughing, without a care in the world, sounds like heaven to most Aries. The ram is equally as comfortable in the grittiest dive bar as they are in the VIP section—they'll go anywhere, as long as the company is good and the vibe is exciting.

RELATIONSHIP APPROACH

No matter the relationship format, monogamous or polyamorous, Aries longs to be number one, so be sure to make your ram feel like they're being put first. Be present with them as they express their feelings: independent Aries doesn't ask for much, but when they do, they need to be able to depend on their partner. Aries are loyal and honest as partners (they'll dump you if they realize they would rather cheat on or lie to you), and they expect the same kind of integrity from the people they are in a relationship with.

Homemaking doesn't come naturally to Aries; however, it's still something they deeply crave, and a partner who can create a home, cook, and help clean is often something that feels like a "missing piece" in Aries's life. Once they find their passion, Aries is serious about their work and needs a partner who is sincerely excited about their success and won't be jealous or competitive. Aries wants a partnership that's a united front, with someone who takes joy in their success . . . if you can't do that, then you're just another jealous hater to the ram!

SEX

Passionate Aries loves to have sex and doesn't want to wait long to do it! They immerse themself fully in sex: loud, hard, dirty, fast, and full of fireworks is typical Aries lovemaking.

Aries is fine with quickies—as long as there are many of them! They don't want to go long between lovemaking sessions, and while a quickie is cool, a night full of passion is still what their heart desires, so make sure to enjoy plenty of long evenings with your ram. They crave fireworks, and a fireworks show that only lasts a few short minutes is lame!

Have a big imagination—sex is a form of escape from the pressures of everyday life for Aries, and they enjoy fantasy between the sheets. That said, opening up about their kinks can be hard for them unless they know you won't judge them, so show yourself to be open-minded. Tough Aries doesn't get a chance to be vulnerable every day, so keep that in mind when they share something private with you!

Aries is the sign that rules the head, and yes, they've got a lot of intense stuff going on in their minds, even if they seem so confident on the outside. Sex is a form of healing for them, and they find lovemaking and its ability to ground them in their bodies and to explore their psyches through role-play highly therapeutic.

TURN-ONS

Be in a state of wonder and awe when you have sex with Aries, and make it seem like everything is your first time. That said, there's no need to pretend you are a virgin (well, actually, that's not a bad role-play idea with Aries!), but saying things like "Wow, I've always been a heartbreaker, but now, for the first time, I want to see where this could go," or "No one has touched me like that before" can really turn them on. But only say these things if you mean them!

Firsts aren't the only things that get them off; being the best is important, too, so let them know how amazing they make you feel.

Aries is very dominant in their everyday life, so surprisingly, in the bedroom they often appreciate being able to give the power to someone else, taking on a more submissive role. A submissive ram is likely to have a bratty side, while a dominant Aries enjoys being the boss, or being royalty, or even being a caretaker in some way. Whatever the role, they'll make you remember that they're in charge.

Hard and fast is how Aries approaches everything, but if you're able to help them slow down and really *feel* what's happening, they'll be putty in your hands. Encourage them to masturbate for you, as they love being the object of someone's attention, especially if you take an active role by caressing their face, kissing them, playing with their nipples, or otherwise lending a hand while you watch them touch themself.

Aries is a size queen, so be sure to get a dildo that's at least larger than average if you are going to get them a sex toy. A whip or riding crop isn't a bad idea, either, as this Mars-ruled sign can certainly get into BDSM. But as thrill-seeking as the ram may be, Aries also has a thing for cuteness, whether that's pigtails, knee socks, or a freshly shaven face (although scruff has its place in Aries's heart, too; it depends on the mood!).

Depending on the vibe, pull or caress their hair while you are fucking them. Aries rules the head, and activating their scalp will go a long way in pleasing them.

TURN-OFFS

Energetic Aries doesn't want a lazy lover. Don't be afraid to be theatrical in bed! If you don't seem turned on, they will be turned off. Grunting and squealing is a good thing in Aries's eyes, and don't tone down your o-face.

Falling asleep immediately after sex without any time to connect can annoy Aries. Aries may be a warrior, but they are still the baby of the zodiac (they're the first sign!), and they want to be held, connected with, and cared for.

Aries wants to be number one, so don't mention any other lovers within a few hours of wanting to get into bed with a ram. That said, if you're in a group sex scenario, Aries absolutely loves to feel like the center of attention, having each part of their body attended to by a different person.

ARIES & ARIES

No one pursues a crush like Aries does, and even the ram themself is taken aback when a fellow Aries swings onto the scene making a grand romantic gesture. Here's the strangest part: Aries is often turned off when someone comes on too strongly. However, when another Aries does it—even if they don't know that person is an Aries—somehow, they're turned on!

They are both very generous people, but they both have anger issues to work out, too. If they are patient, forgiving, and able to commit to improving themselves (which isn't a hard promise for Aries since self-improvement is genuinely something they strive for), then this relationship can have lasting power. But it is fun just as a fling, too! Although Aries genuinely believes in self-improvement, sometimes it takes a few tries to get them to see it all the way through. Their ability to believe in each other totally, through good times and bad, while appreciating and being empathetic toward each other's flaws and challenges, creates a strong friendship between these two.

Sex proves to be a deeply transformative experience for them by opening the door to either exploring new turn-ons or rethinking their approach to lovemaking. Together they are good with money for the most part; however, they can't help but give in to each other's desire for luxuries. Their home is a cozy retreat from the outside world—let's just hope this reckless bunch doesn't start any fires in the kitchen!

ARIES & TAURUS

Do they like me, or not?! the impatient Aries wonders as their slow-moving crush deliberates their feelings. One thing is for sure: Aries moves much faster than Taurus! Taurus will need to catch up if they're interested, or else Aries may move on. Aries should try to slow down a bit, too. It will be Aries who has to compromise, but it's a good thing when they do: these two signs will find that they share a riotous sense of humor.

Taurus is in awe of Aries's spontaneity and willpower. The ram is a total mystery to Taurus, and their relationship encourages them to explore hidden or repressed sides of themself. Brave and confident Aries surprisingly finds that sometimes Taurus stirs insecurity in them. Issues concerning security and finances are some of the lessons Aries learns from Taurus, a sign who's very conscious of wealth and security.

Aries shows Taurus things they could never have imagined in bed, while Taurus teaches Aries to slow down and savor the moment. As a one-night stand, the energy is very intense—Taurus might even tell Aries that they have been waiting so long to get between the sheets with them, which of course will shock the ram, who has been trying to get them there for who knows how long! If they decide to move in together, Taurus won't mind cooking, but Aries will certainly have to clean *and* give a back rub, too. If they get into an argument, Aries will need to learn that their temper isn't going to get them anywhere. One of my first bosses, who was a Taurus, used to tell me (an Aries), "You catch more flies with honey than with vinegar," whenever I was struggling with my angry ram attitude. The same is true for catching bulls and cows.

ARIES & GEMINI

Aries is so grateful to meet someone as straightforward as Gemini—not to mention, so polite and conscientious! It inspires them to act politely, too. Anyone who can be a good influence on Aries, the impulsive and rambunctious baby of the zodiac, is sure to be fantastic. There are, of course, some Geminis who fib, and if the ram catches one doing so, the relationship will end swiftly and Aries will move on to someone new. The ram despises insincerity and hates being bullshitted. Of course, Aries will need to behave, too. Aries's anger can freak out nervous Gemini, causing them to split quickly if the vibe gets cross.

If the twins and the ram are a little more mature, this can be a fantastic relationship—best friends who do everything together, yet still give each other all the space they need to do their own thing. They both value independence and are very fun people. Gemini's brilliant imagination and communication skills are incredibly attractive to Aries, while Gemini just thinks Aries is straight-up cool. Aries would be wise to stay optimistic and open-minded around Gemini if they really want to win them over, and Gemini would be smart to show how nurturing they can be.

Gemini's versatility in bed keeps Aries excited, and with Gemini, Aries feels comfortable asking for their wildest dreams to come true between the sheets. Their home is a retreat from the busy outside world and should have space for them both to have their own offices. Close proximity to nature would be helpful, too. A walk in the woods clears Gemini's busy mind and helps Aries unwind and release tension. Whether they're in nature, under the stars, or in the middle of a crowded dance floor, when these two lock eyes and their hands graze each other's, sparks fly. It's the magic, the electric connection they've both been waiting for. It might be unexpected, but it's undeniable.

ARIES & CANCER

If the ram and crab can move past their very different ways of doing things—the ram's straightforward head butting versus Cancer's side-to-side shuffle—these two can engage in a truly fairy-tale romance. They can learn a lot from their differences; in fact, the tension that takes place between these two creates fantastic sexual chemistry—Cancer's nurturing and emotionally tuned-in energy combined with Aries's presence and power makes for an evening neither will soon forget.

It's rare these two can have a simple, one-night fling, but it can happen (though the memory will last a long time!). If these two break up, it's likely there will be some on-again, off-again smooching. If they decide to move in together, Cancer builds the home Aries always longed for, while the ram encourages the crab to chase after their career dreams—the ram's confidence rubs off on the crab in a splendid way.

Aries doesn't mind Cancer's moods (it makes Aries more curious about them, if anything), but if Cancer never wants to socialize with any of Aries's friends—or worse, doesn't want to introduce Aries to their social circle—Aries will feel snubbed. Aries would be wise to grow up—yes, they are the baby of the zodiac, but Cancer needs a partner who can handle adult issues maturely and confidently. All that said, no one holds Aries like a Cancer can... and no one empowers Cancer to chase their dreams like Aries does.

This can be a powerful couple, if they're both ready for it. Aries's fearless nature is empowering and inspiring to the crab, who has lived a life building a hard exterior against the hardships life can bring... and Cancer's nurturing abilities soothe Aries after long days fighting for their shared dreams.

ARIES & LEO

Aries's spark brings just the drama that Leo longs for. Can the most regal sign in the zodiac and Aries, a sign who's all about being number one, share the spotlight? Absolutely! The best only want to spend time with the best, right? Aries can get caught off guard by Leo's demands, and the lion can sometimes feel left out of Aries's itinerary, but these two Fire signs are sure to have an exciting time. Leo would be wise to be more flexible than they usually are when they're with Aries, and Aries would be smart to be a little more aloof and not so straightforward or obvious about their affection for Leo, because Leo loves to pursue as much as Aries does.

Ultimately, Aries deeply appreciates Leo's dependability, and Leo is inspired by the many late-night conversations they share about everything from politics to spirituality to gossiping about friends. The sex is as good as their ability to communicate their needs, which often means it's phenomenal! But, if their kinks don't align, they'll likely lose interest quickly, perhaps keeping things casual for make-out sessions on yachts or after late-night parties.

If they decide to live together, their home will be warm and cozy, a place to recharge and hide away from the outside world—they're both more private than they would seem (especially Leo, who loves the spotlight . . . but what star doesn't value their privacy?!).

ARIES & VIRGO

Both are straightforward, no-bullshit people—to Aries, this is natural; to Virgo, it might be too good to be true. *How could someone be so honest? There must be something else going on,* they'll wonder. Once they move past any initial testing Virgo does of Aries's trustworthiness, and if Virgo doesn't hold the ram to unfair double standards, these two will be great friends and lovers.

Virgo challenges Aries to be more responsible and take care of their health, while Aries pushes Virgo to confront emotional issues they may have been avoiding or unaware of and forces them to take intimacy to a new level. Both signs are always questing to know themselves better, so they're sure to share many late nights musing over the meaning of a tarot spread they pulled together. But they have different approaches—Aries is on a search for self-knowledge because all they are aware of *is* themself, while Virgo is very aware of the people around them and their needs, often wondering, *Who are they?*

This relationship demands self-reflection, and if Aries doesn't have the attention span, or if Virgo is busy with too many other side projects, the partnership may fall apart. But they share a sense of adventure and believe tomorrow is a new day, where, if they had failed to connect in the past, they can always try again. Virgo knows practice makes perfect, and Aries isn't up for losing or wallowing. Awkward moments are sure to take place, but both signs know that growing pains often come with progress.

ARIES & LIBRA

Libra isn't one for conformation. When they meet the ram, they'll find someone who is happy to take on all their battles! And Aries learns a lot about staying cool, logical, and diplomatic from Libra. Aries is happy to make all the decisions for indecisive Libra, but Aries needs to be careful not to be overbearing. They are opposites on the zodiac wheel and complement each other beautifully, but there is a unique chemistry between them that makes them feel like they're embarking on love for the first time (which is unlikely with flirtatious Libra and impulsive Aries). But when they connect, if they start to fall in love, they do wonder if they had ever been in love before they met each other.

There are, of course, a few things that could prevent a deep love from taking hold. They're likely to keep things very casual if Aries notices Libra flirting with everyone in the room (Aries needs to feel like they are number one or else they lose interest), or if Libra feels this ram has too short an attention span and can't finish anything they start doing.

In general, these two are able to be honest with each other about their needs, and their needs match one another's, which bodes well for their relationship. These two make a great team. Relationship-oriented Libra supports Aries, while Aries encourages Libra to do their own thing, fearlessly.

The energy between the sheets is magnetic—Libra loves to feel beautiful and to please their partner, and Aries knows how to make someone feel completely desirable and appreciates an adventurous person. If they decide to move in with each other, Libra should be the one to handle the paperwork and deal with realtors (they have more patience for people), and Aries should handle packing all their things—Aries needs physical outlets to blow off steam!

ARIES & SCORPIO

The rambunctious ram and the strategic scorpion have a lot in common: both are ruled by Mars, both love to fuck, and both like to pick fights—they need to be careful and choose their battles wisely! There's plenty of drama in store for these two, but hey, they kind of like it that way. These two signs are both committed to self-development, and together they will enjoy exploring spirituality, sexuality, and the meaning and purpose of life.

For the long haul, Aries needs to watch out about being bossy, and Scorpio needs to learn how to let go of a grudge and forgive and forget. Aries's temper tantrums won't take them far, but neither will any of Scorpio's manipulations. Aries is too impulsive to be a good target for any tricks Scorpio might have up their sleeve. If these two can't

be tender with each other, it's not a pairing that's worth the time for either of them.

But when they're loving and supportive, Aries is able to teach Scorpio a lot about how to achieve their goals and how to manage their time and energy, and Scorpio will encourage Aries to face their fears. Fierce Aries is very brave, but Scorpio can see the inner child within them who might still need a hug.

The energy between the sheets is powerful: when Scorpio's intensity in the bedroom meets Aries's passion, there are sure to be fireworks. If they decide to move in together, they'll likely have more sex toys and props than anything else in their apartment! A sauna and steam room would be a plus, too.

ARIES & SAGITTARIUS

Aries and Sagittarius are both Fire signs, which means they have a strong will and passionate nature in common; however, they do have a lot to learn from each other. The way they go about things it quite different—but not incompatible! For instance, Sagittarius, the archer, shoots its target from far away, while the ram bashes into it with its horns. Sagittarius looks at the big picture, while Aries smashes its face into things. However, Aries is inspired by Sagittarius's mind, philosophy, and worldview; Sagittarius is in awe of Aries's bravery and spontaneity. Sagittarius might have a more sophisticated way of shooting a target, but Aries is real, raw, and fierce—and Sag respects it.

This pairing is fantastic as a fling, and fiery marathon sex is likely; their open way of communicating means they can ask each other for anything without hesitation. These two can also stay friends after their affair. If it's more long term, Aries will continue to be inspired by Sagittarius's intellect and thirst for knowledge, while Aries keeps things fresh and fun for pleasure-seeking Sag. Sagittarius loves to party, and Aries always seems to know where the best action is; plus, Aries's spontaneous nature is endlessly appealing to Sagittarius, who respects routine but is really happiest when things are kept fresh.

If they decide to move in together, they'll likely expand their relationship to include more creative projects to work on with each other, as well as cultivate their spiritual practices—they both have plenty of books on philosophy and spiritual wisdom from around the world that they'll enjoy sharing together.

ARIES & CAPRICORN

The relationship between the ram and the sea goat is one that spans decades—whether they're together as a long-term couple or run into each other here and there for hookups, flings, and coffee dates, these two seem to meet again and again. And every time, they ask each other (out loud, or maybe just in their minds), "Who have I become since I've seen you last?" and "How are my feelings for you gaining new dimensions, yet staying solidly, somehow, the same?"

Their time in the bedroom is very passionate and physical, as they both release—and reveal—themselves fully, and often have a lusty, deep attraction to each other that can't be quenched by anyone else. Aries is feisty yet sincere, which is so attractive to Capricorn, while Aries feels a big ego boost from knowing that they meet Capricorn's high standards.

Capricorn is who Aries wants to be when they grow up, which might take a while, as Aries is the infant of the zodiac. Aries, though not the most domestic sign on the zodiac wheel, manages to create a warm home for Capricorn, who, though perhaps a workaholic, really craves a safe, secure space to retreat into. Capricorn would be wise to be sensitive to Aries, who needs a lot of open affection from their partners. "Warm" and "cuddly" are not the first two words used to describe Capricorns, but they certainly have that side to them—we are all human—and bringing it out for the Aries they love will take this relationship very far. As for Aries, they too need to reveal their nurturing side. Aries is fiercely protective of the people they love, and that's the quality that Capricorn loves about them most.

ARIES & AQUARIUS

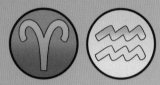

Aquarius is one of the coolest people Aries has ever met, and the feeling is mutual: Aquarius is struck by how Aries seems to know everyone. These two make great friends, and both need some space in a relationship to be comfortable. However, they also both thrive on verbal affirmation, spontaneity, and plenty of communication.

Aquarius's cool-headed vibe is soothing to hothead Aries, and Aquarius is charmed by Aries's ability to stay optimistic even in hard times. Aries isn't afraid of being a show-off and should certainly flaunt their talents and love of the spotlight to Aquarius, who loves an entertaining and outgoing partner. Aquarius would be wise to loosen up and be a little more flexible—Aries loves how dependable they are, but not how rigid they can be. Aquarius is known for being aloof; however, because the two have so much fun, the ram doesn't recognize this as distant . . . until, one

day, they do, and sadness strikes Aries's heart. Honest communication is important for these two—things move so quickly that they both miss the "what is this?" conversation.

Aquarius knows that the future may hold amazing things, and Aries's ability to make things happen turns them on. They have fantastic sexual banter, and if they decide to stick together and move in, their home will be much comfier than people would expect. Their fridge will always be stocked with a few indulgences. They have an enviable sex toy collection, and if they're just friends who hook up casually, they'll have a blast attending sex parties together or otherwise exploring their interests and desires. Sharing their mushy, sentimental feelings for each other is sure to be a thrill, as neither sign shows their softer side to people very often.

ARIES & PISCES

This pair shares big laughs and big adventures but will also need to overcome big insecurities. Shy Pisces is emboldened by Aries's presence—they know the ram will stick up for them should they run into trouble during one of their escapades. Being around Aries inspires them to think of themself as great, and Aries thinks so of themself and Pisces, too. That said, there are instances where Aries's in-your-face attitude may scare off a fish, but if sexual attraction trumps Pisces's fear of confrontation, this pair will gain a lot from spending time together. Aries is totally mystified by Pisces, which may stir insecurity in them—Aries can have a very hard time reading the fish, so it's important these two communicate with each other. It's also important that they are clear on their own and each other's boundaries, and that they don't indulge paranoid thoughts.

They do, however, have a riotous sense of humor with each other and are eager to explore whatever places the other is interested in. Once they get over the hump of getting to know each other, these two will become amazing friends and lovers, whether it's casual or committed. If they decide to move in together, their home will have a whimsical yet cozy energy.

Pisces is a fantastic listener, helping Aries work out deep issues that weigh on their mind. Aries gives Pisces fantastic pep talks, encouraging them to chase after what they want. Their energy in bed is dreamy and intense, as Aries's fire and Pisces's empathy create a unique passion that they can't find with anyone else. Aries is the first sign of the zodiac and Pisces is the last— they complete the circle, and so their relationship is sure to be a heavy one.

TAURUS

THE BULL

DATES: APRIL 20-MAY 21

PLANETARY RULER: VENUS
ELEMENT: EARTH
MODALITY: FIXED

PERSONALITY

Taurus is not in a rush. Taurus is focused on the present. Like a cow that serenely sits under the rays of the warm Sun in a field of heather, Taurus takes their time to recognize and appreciate life's pleasures. What a wonderful moment to *be* in the moment.

Ruled by Venus, Taurus explores pleasure through the five senses. From tasty meals to luxurious fabrics, Taurus wants the best from this world. Money and beauty, too, are important in Taurus's realm.

As the first Earth sign on the zodiac wheel, Taurus is attracted to the material realm, and as a *fixed* sign (the middle sign of a season, in this instance, spring), Taurus is just that: fixed. Some would say stubborn, others might say persistent. But without their diligent perseverance, how could development ever take place?

Fertile Taurus's energy is massively creative. What fantastic things may be born from Taurus's secure sphere? One must wait and see, because things may move slowly in Taurus's world, but that doesn't mean you won't be surprised!

AT THEIR BEST

Stylish and luxurious, Taurus has wonderful taste and wants to surround themselves and the people they love with beautiful objects, delicious food, and opulent environments. Their generous and sumptuous spending is offset by their fiscally responsible nature.

They generally have a relaxed attitude (unless you wave a red flag in their face, but to be fair, that would annoy anyone).

Peaceful Taurus is not looking to pick a fight, just for some delicious snacks. Creative and inventive, Taurus typically has many valuable talents for any team. Despite their love for lounging about, they tend to be quite productive. Taurus's unwavering, determined, and steadfast attitude makes them a reliable and hard worker, and loyal to their friends and family.

AT THEIR WORST

Taurus will often lose interest in astrology after reading that they are stubborn—and of course, in true Taurus fashion, they *never* read their horoscope again. Because they are so inflexible, compromise isn't something that comes naturally to Taurus; however, possessiveness does. They are persistent—annoyingly so. They can also be materialistic, greedy, grumpy, and boring to be around, and they'll respond to your questions with monosyllabic answers if they're upset. Will they dump you? No, that would require change, which is something Taurus just doesn't do too often. Until, of course, they've been pushed over their edge—then run, because a charging bull is a scary sight, indeed!

LOVE PERSONALITY

Taurus values objects and relationships that last. These creatures of habit crave security and peaceful surroundings. They are romantic, bestowing their loved ones with gifts, yet they are realistic and smart with their money (at least most of the time). They tend to be serial monogamists, until they realize that something needs to change. In polyamorous relationships, they are very dependable partners. Before committing, Taurus truly takes the time to get to know their partner, because once they enter a relationship—polyamorous or not—they can become stuck in it; change doesn't come easily to this fixed sign.

So, what is Taurus looking for? They crave a partner whom they can see themself in—physically and intellectually. If they can look through someone's closet and want to wear their clothes, then that's a great start to a happy match. Art, music, and food are all important aspects of the Taurus life, and they want it to be a big part of their partner's, too—with matching tastes, ideals, and values.

FIRST IMPRESSIONS

For a sign who has a considerable number of name-brand items in their closet and knows the best gourmet restaurants, Taurus is surprisingly down-to-earth. They have an aura of unshakability. Always stylish and put together, Taurus doesn't always go with the flow per se, but they let the flow go on around them: they are an unwavering mountain—standing strong as the world spins. All the chaos in the world can be going on around them, but as long as they're left in peace while they enjoy a soak in the tub, they are content.

They can come across as rather conservative, formal, or even uptight, but don't be fooled. They love a "bad boy/girl," and might even secretly be one themself. Well-made clothing is important to them, and you can bet their outfits are thoughtfully curated. A clothing store is a likely place to run into Taurus. Even if they don't intend on buying anything, they just love feeling silk or cashmere as they mindlessly flip through the racks—a truly meditative sport for Taurus. Music shops, jewelry stores, specialty bakeries, and art supply stores are also great places to run into them; Taurus is creative and enjoys being surrounded with beauty.

FLIRTING TECHNIQUES

Food is a fantastic icebreaker when it comes to Taurus. If you meet them online, ask them about the last amazing restaurant they went to, and where you both should go (they love introducing people to places they are excited about). Cool and laid-back, Taurus might appear to be aloof or uncomplicated; however, they are most attracted to deep thinkers and extreme people who have had complicated pasts, tell exciting stories, and aren't afraid of danger, so show this side of yourself.

Friendship and communication are also important to them, so ask them about their day as often as you send a nude. Even a Taurus who is only looking for a fuck buddy wants their partners to be thoughtful communicators. Don't be too aggressive in your approach, as Taurus is attracted to people who are mysterious. They love intense people; however, if you're pushy it will be a big turn-off. You'll know Taurus likes you because they'll include you in their routine: a sweet text in the morning, or perhaps coffee dates each Tuesday at lunch.

DATING STYLE

As an Earth sign and nature lover, Taurus would enjoy a leisurely stroll through the botanical garden, a picnic in the park, or relaxing in a hammock. Food is very important to Taurus, as is art, and of course, music. Anything that awakens the senses is big for Taurus, so visiting a gallery, going to a concert, and trying a new restaurant are all fantastic date ideas. Go shopping! They love a partner who will talk about fashion, albums, or whatever they're currently collecting.

Taurus is a hard worker, so laying back and being lazy is definitely their favorite way to unwind, and they enjoy indulging, whether with a joint, a drink, or gourmet chocolates.

Note: While Taurus may absolutely love getting high (April 20 is the first day of the Taurus season), some may be more comfortable staying grounded in reality. So before offering your Taurus friend a puff or a drink, get to know them first! Taurus never wants to feel like a party pooper, so ask them what their limits are early on. Otherwise, you may end up with a sad Taurus who is uncomfortable that they had to deny you a good time.

RELATIONSHIP APPROACH

Security, emotional and financial, is very important to Taurus. They value having steady income, safe surroundings, and a set schedule (as well as autonomy—they don't need someone telling them what to do and when), and they want to partner with someone who also has their shit together. Better yet: be someone who they'd want to be.

Steadfast Taurus knows what they want—and they don't like to try new things. If monogamy is their thing, that's their thing. If they prefer open relationships, that's how it will be. Don't try to change them. Many people enter relationships subconsciously believing they can change their partner—don't do this with Taurus. Not only will you not be able to get them to change, but they'll also be offended if you try to mold them into what you want rather than supporting and encouraging them.

Taurus is looking for a powerful partner: someone who keeps the mystery going and isn't afraid to deal with the more difficult or scary parts of life, such as finances, intimacy, and endings. Change isn't easy for Taurus, so they need someone they can lean on and help them recover during turbulent times. As an Earth sign—a very physical element—gift giving is certainly important; however, helping them with chores or otherwise making their lives easier (and allowing them to relax) is highly valuable to them. If your Taurus lover is giving you the silent treatment, remember how important touch is to them: a hug can help when communication fails. And remember: Taurus is always right! (At least in their mind!)

SEX

Sex with a Taurus is a time to slow down and to connect with your senses. Taurus typically has a playlist to go with lovemaking, and if you set out a spread of snacks for them to munch on between sex acts, you will certainly make an impression. Feed them foods that act as aphrodisiacs, like chocolate and chile-infused snacks!

Taurus can be very picky about how they like the scene set for lovemaking—pay attention to how they set the scene when you first hook up for clues on how to make it comfortable for them the next time. For example, if they turn on a fan, make sure to have a fan in your space also, so Taurus won't get all sweaty! Or, if they need a glass of something to drink right afterward, take note, and remember to have one ready for them the next time. Taurus loves romance, but they don't necessarily need candles and flowers for it to be perfect. Instead, focus on providing a clean and comfortable space that caters to their specific preferences—and that's something you can only learn by getting to know them!

They enjoy being teased—the longer you can draw out the lovemaking session, the better! They can certainly be dominant in bed; however, they also deeply enjoy being ravished and having someone else take the lead. They want to be adored, caressed, and pampered.

TURN-ONS

Taurus rules the neck, so kiss and lick them gently there—but don't leave a mark! They probably have a job that they need to be presentable for!

Dirty talk also gets them going. A dirty secret whispered directly in their ear is fantastic, but it's not just what you say, but also the autonomous sensory meridian response (ASMR) that comes with lightly breathing and whispering into their ear. Taurus is all about the senses.

My teacher, astrologer Anne Ortelee, taught me some valuable advice about sleeping with a Taurus: tie them up and plow them (this advice also applies to the other cloven members of the zodiac!). Branding them, perhaps getting matching tattoos, or giving them a collar is some other wisdom I gleaned from Ortelee.

Ownership is a theme associated with materially minded Earth sign Taurus: dominant Taurus gets off on power and control. Taurus loves *objects*—beautiful lingerie, luxury sex toys, and silk bedding are a must. Sex toys, such as beautiful, well-made harnesses, should also be on the shopping list. The submissive Taurus revels with an imaginative partner—they want to be taken on a journey. Creativity in bed is important to Taurus, as they long for a partner who can explore the psychological aspects of lovemaking with them.

Sensual, tactile Taurus likes to be physically stimulated. Have tools for teasing, such as feathers, or for massage, like a vibrator (for genital stimulation or for another body part) and massage oil. Taurus wants to feel good all over! They're especially turned on by someone who keeps things suspenseful—tease them by asking if they know what you plan to do for them in bed later, and keep the energy mounting by having them hold off on climax.

TURN-OFFS

Don't expect to get into bed with a Taurus after you have looked through their phone, handbag, or drawers. They want to feel trusted, and their privacy is very important to them.

Taurus is not looking to try uncomfortable or acrobatic sex positions. If one sign can lie around all day, doing nothing but fucking, it's certainly Taurus, but the key phrase here is *lie around all day.*

Safety first for Taurus: Safe sex is important no matter which sign you are fucking, but Taurus wants to discuss getting tested and using protection early on. If you're one of those who is indifferent about using protection, expect Taurus to be totally turned off. Sharing body fluids is a big deal to Taurus.

TAURUS & ARIES

There's something dangerous, even mysterious (as straightforward as the ram may be), about Aries to Taurus. Aries adds so much excitement to their lives, yet are total enigmas to them! How can someone be so forward yet so hard to read?

For Aries, the experience of wooing a Taurus can be rough. Taurus just moves so slowly, and Aries isn't used to it. But in the bedroom, this slow pace is actually quite nice! Taurus is all about teaching Aries how to slow down and actually *feel* what's happening between the sheets. Their energy in bed is a blend of Taurus's sensuality and Aries's fire—a different pace for each of them than they're used to, but sometimes change is just what someone needs.

Aries shouldn't be afraid to open up to Taurus and share a secret or two, and Taurus should make an effort to compromise with Aries, especially if they want to win their trust. Aries pushes Taurus to explore hidden parts of themselves that immovable Taurus would be content to leave unexamined. Together, they share a fantastic sense of humor: even talking about boring, everyday stuff is enjoyable for them. In fact, Aries learns a lot about how to take care of themselves practically and financially from Taurus.

If they decide to move in together, their home will be a cozy one. Taurus will ensure that their home will be well kept, with beautiful objects and high-end fabrics. Aries just needs to promise to ensure Taurus's favorite snacks are kept in stock. But as long as these two signs can continue to keep their passion going, they will be able to laugh and have fun in the bedroom and out.

TAURUS & TAURUS

When two bulls meet, it might take a while for things to get off the ground, but the solid friendship they build is worth it. They usually have shared interests, and the best indication that things will work out is if they can look through each other's closets and see themselves in their partner's clothes. Taste is important to Taurus; not because they are shallow, but because they engage through their senses, which color their whole experience.

It's important that these two motivate each other. They can get in ruts and need to be with a person who can encourage them to try something new. They both long to be innovators in their fields, and at home, they both carve an opulent, luxurious space.

They enjoy having a routine with their partner: a time to check in, places they enjoy regularly, and little traditions—or superstitions—they can share. At times they'll attempt to out-stubborn one another, but it's more likely that they'll totally forget that they were at a standoff before they give in to one another.

These two can lounge in bed all day, lazily moving from sex to breakfast to cuddling to lunch to more sex. At any one time, their bed will either be a mess of sex toys or a pile of clothes (and hopefully not takeout breakfast, lunch, and/or dinner). Don't put it past this couple to eat in bed, even though they have a gorgeous dining room table that one of them might have made by hand from reclaimed wood—yes, Taurus has a reputation for being lazy, but when they get to work, beautiful things are made.

TAURUS & GEMINI

There is no one Gemini is more bewildered by than Taurus. Gemini—curious, chatty, and often full of nerves—looks at chill, peaceful Taurus and wonders how the hell someone can achieve such an untroubled state of mind. Of course, Taurus has plenty of things on their mind (security, for example), and there is something about Gemini's easygoing nature that jabs at Taurus's self-esteem—Gemini is so light and airy! Spending more than a one-night fling with Gemini is sure to leave Taurus wondering whether they can keep up with someone so flexible, witty, and cool (the answer is yes, and dear Taurus should never try to change their ways for anyone—it's against their nature, anyway).

They'll have an adventurous sex life, and while Taurus usually isn't itching to break from their routines, they'll have a fun time doing it with versatile Gemini, who brings an electric energy

to bed. Taurus would be wise to show how artistic and cultured they are—Gemini loves being around someone creative who knows about arts and culture. Gemini should reveal their inquisitive nature, as well as help boost Taurus's confidence—a compliment from cool Gemini goes a very long way with Taurus.

If it's just a short fling, it will be especially hot if it's secret in nature—Gemini loves anything where they have to try not to get caught, and Taurus is turned on by intrigue (their daily routine can be pretty mundane, as they love security so). If they choose to move in together, they'll need to make room for Taurus to lounge like royalty, as well as a space for Gemini to work—Gemini's restlessness can be a bit annoying to chill Taurus, but as long as Gemini can offer the stability and loyalty Taurus craves, these two can find happiness!

TAURUS & CANCER

The Taurus and Cancer pair reading this book together has certainly had the following discussion about astrology:

Taurus: "You know, I'm not sure I believe in astrology; all my horoscopes say I'm stubborn."

Cancer: "Yes, and they all say I'm moody and obsessed with my mom. I don't think that's fair!"

Others may call these out as "flaws," but these two are drawn to those traits. Taurus doesn't find Cancer to be moody and doesn't think there's anything wrong with talking about your family. Taurus's need for security and a comfortable home is a great match with Cancer's love of a familial life. Taurus thinks the crab leads a full and busy life, with things to do, choices to make, places to go—of course, with so much

going on, there will be moods (by the way, their favorite shared mood is "hungry"). Cancer doesn't think of Taurus as stubborn, but as dependable—and also very, very cool. They admire Taurus for their knowledge of art and culture and for having a unique vision about what the future holds.

These two are best friends and passionate lovers: Cancer's imagination meets Taurus's sensuality for hours of pleasure. They do, however, have to watch out for any passive-aggressive attitudes. They might go weeks without talking as they try to outdo each other with silence. If they're able to commit and decide to move in together, their home will be luxurious, filled with rustic touches, and very cozy. The kitchen will be busy, for sure!

TAURUS & LEO

When Taurus and Leo have their hearts set on something, they're determined to see it through—but will they fix their sights on this relationship? This union is fun as a fling—spotlight-loving Leo enjoys being out with sexy Taurus, and Taurus feels cozy around Leo's warm aura. A touch of jealousy adds some drama to this union, but if they're up-front and honest with each other, a little drama won't deter these two.

Long term, Taurus finds someone they can build a home with in Leo, and Leo is inspired by Taurus's determination and creativity, stirring them to chase their dreams even harder. Taurus is typically drawn to broodier types than Leo, but Leo's sunny nature can be astoundingly refreshing to Taurus. Leo, too, usually has a different type, typically attracted to someone wackier, more out there than seemingly buttoned-up Taurus, but Taurus has a way of surprising people.

These two will often find each other when they're ready for a great change, and they'll take action to shake things up. Leo's flair for glamour combined with Taurus's lusty energy for a good time brings the passion into the bedroom time and again. This could be an on-and-off affair, but if they decide to stick together, they'll discover sides of themselves that they couldn't have imagined seeing. If they live together, Taurus might get a glimpse of how spiritual Leo is—Taurus may be surprised to know Leo likes to take walks alone to pray. And Leo will learn how creative Taurus really is. Although Taurus isn't usually the first to volunteer during karaoke, Leo's heart may be filled with pride for their beloved after hearing Taurus in the shower.

TAURUS & VIRGO

They might both be Earth signs, but they are very different: Luxury-loving Taurus has an entire closet full of plush towels and Egyptian cotton sheets, while Virgo just has a neat drawer with the necessities. Virgo saves their hard-earned cash by cooking a meal at home that meets their nutritional needs, while Taurus is having a free-for-all at a buffet.

In the garden, Taurus lounges on the hammock, while Virgo weeds . . . but they'll still enjoy each other's company, with Taurus reading something interesting to Virgo from the hammock, and Virgo tending to the rosebush that Taurus loves so much. Virgo is inspired by Taurus's intellect, which Taurus appreciates (because, you know, it's

been hard for Taurus to feel like people think they're smart when everyone just notices how cute their outfit is!). And with Virgo, Taurus has plenty of fun (and believe me, Virgo is very critical about what constitutes "fun"!).

If they want to impress each other, Virgo would be wise to reveal their kinkier side, and Taurus should share a strange dream they had with analytical Virgo so they can try their hand at interpreting it. In the bedroom, they crave physical pleasure as much as emotional intimacy. If they're more than just a fling and they decide to move in together, they'll agree on most things—besides the quality or quantity of snacks in the kitchen.

TAURUS & LIBRA

Taurus and Libra love the good things in life, but all the luxury in the world won't keep these two from eventually having one of the most intense relationships of their lives. Even if their union is just a short fling, Taurus's presence in Libra's life triggers deep changes and transformations, and Libra will leave forever changed. Taurus goes through some growing pains with Libra, too, learning just how important a work-life balance is, and the importance of maintaining their health and well-being.

Around Libra, Taurus is pushed to put an end to bad habits, which will be hard, because Libra shares Taurus's same vices: shopping, having too good a time with friends, and mindlessly swiping on dating apps just to see what cuties are out there! Things work best when Libra shows off their strategic, savvy side to Taurus, and Taurus takes on a more go-getter attitude, rather than being passive.

Mirrors and cameras are welcome in the bedroom as these two vain Venusian lovers will adore seeing themselves through the lens of their lover's camera. Plenty of toys will litter their space, too. If they live together, they'll need a *lot* of room: they both have tons of clothes, with Taurus's side of the closet filled with vintage finds and Libra's filled with trendy pieces.

Libra's ideal night out is a fun dinner at a new and exciting restaurant, followed by a night dancing with their beloved and their friends, which is a sharp contrast to the comfort food Taurus plans to enjoy on their back porch during a beautiful quiet sunset . . . but there is something these two Venusian lovers both crave: harmony. Peace is so important to these two, and if they love each other, they will find it.

TAURUS & SCORPIO

These two look like a match made in heaven in many ways—Scorpio needs a partner they can depend on, and Taurus is seeking depth—but they both need to be honest about what they are looking for and respect each other's boundaries.

Scorpio craves a solid, strong partner—not much in this world is guaranteed, and a partner who they can trust is crucial to them, but that doesn't mean they're not looking for excitement. Scorpio perfectly encapsulates what Taurus usually looks for—a bit secretive, passionate, and cultured. However, Scorpio's sometimes overwhelming emotions are something Taurus may not be prepared for. These two will need to be careful not to get stuck in ruts. Taurus is looking for depth, and they'll find plenty of that in Scorpio.

They can both be possessive, so they'll have to be smart about discussing this issue, as ironically, neither likes to feel smothered. Sensual Taurus helps brooding Scorpio stay in the moment and not get lost within their own thoughts, and Scorpio is down for exploring all the kinky acts Taurus is itching to do in bed. Even a short fling between these two will be intense and lustful. If they decide to share a home together, Taurus should be the one to decide their surroundings and décor, and Scorpio, being the detective of the zodiac, should handle the safety and security precautions for their home.

TAURUS & SAGITTARIUS

"Comfortable" is one of Taurus's favorite words, but they'll have to confront some discomfort with Sagittarius, whether that's tight legroom on an airplane or deep conversations about everything from sex to spirituality that challenge Taurus to get out of their comfort zone. Change is inevitable for these two if they're going to stick together for more than a fling (though a fling will prove to be an exciting and sexually indulgent adventure!).

Sagittarius will have to get used to some discomfort, too, including learning how to cope with someone else's routine, as well as getting organized. These challenges could, however, be just what these two are looking for—growth is one of the benefits of relationships, after all. Sagittarius just needs to be patient with Taurus, who takes their time to adjust to new situations, and Taurus should be mindful of Sagittarius's need to keep things moving!

In Taurus, Sagittarius finds security that they didn't know they could ever enjoy, and in Sagittarius, Taurus finds someone they can express their fears to, unlike with anyone else they've ever met. Flexibility is hard for Taurus, but they need to find joy in compromise if they want to impress Sagittarius. As for Sagittarius, being a little less rowdy and a little more incognito when adventuring with Taurus would be appreciated. In bed, they share a love of abundance—lots of champagne, lots of toys, lots of love. If they move in together, Sagittarius should let Taurus do whatever they want to the place, because Taurus will be the one spending more time in it!

TAURUS & CAPRICORN

Taurus is in love with Capricorn's intelligence: the sea goat has been around the block and seen a few things, and Taurus wants to know all about it! What does Capricorn see in Taurus? Taurus knows how to have a good time and how to feel good—things Capricorn certainly wants to enjoy, too, but may have a hard time gifting to themself. But with Taurus, a warm hug, a delicious meal, and a much-needed massage are readily available.

Even if it's just a fling, these two will find a way to linger around each other as long as possible. Long term, the energy is easy, although Capricorn may get annoyed if they feel Taurus isn't ambitious enough. Taurus, in turn, may get ticked off by Capricorn's some-times black-and-white way of looking at things (and Capricorn, in turn, will be really annoyed that Taurus has

called their deep thoughts black and white!). At least they'll get along in the bedroom, where these two Earth signs often find themselves on the same wavelength, craving emotional intimacy but also seeking to explore physical pleasures, with all the toys, lingerie, and kinky trinkets their favorite sex shop has to offer.

Venus, Taurus's ruling planet, is the planet of love and beauty, peace and harmony. It seems to be a very different energy than Capricorn's ruling planet, Saturn, which is the planet of hard work, time, and limits. But, these two planets, and these two signs, have something special in common beneath the surface: Venus rules value, and Saturn, reality. Authenticity—something *real*—is what they're both looking for, and Taurus and Capricorn may just find it together.

TAURUS & AQUARIUS

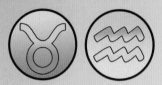

Aquarius is the rebel of the zodiac, so it may not seem like they care about dependability or stability the way Taurus does. But they do! Having their space *and* freedom while still enjoying a stable partnership is totally Aquarius's idea of a perfect relationship. Even when Aquarius is just looking for a fling, they find themself most attracted to a partner who exudes power and strength.

Taurus would do well to show the side of themself that enjoys a little bit of drama in order to keep Aquarius intrigued. Aquarius, in turn, should open up emotionally—show Taurus what's *really* going on underneath! Aquarius might be surprised at what a good listener Taurus truly is, and they may be able to work through a whole lot of emotional processing together!

Their home has plenty of luxurious and DIY touches, but even if these two don't engage in something long term, a fling is just as fun, and may lead to an exciting friendship where they share everything from cooking recipes to phone numbers for recruiters at work—that is, as long as they don't get into any heated arguments early on, because these two might be too stubborn to try to work it out!

Together, with Aquarius's electric spark and Taurus's slow and sensual vibe, they'll likely surprise each other in bed. Communication is key for making things work in bed and out: Aquarius will need to talk slowly and kindly to their Taurus love, and Taurus needs to try not to jump to conclusions or assume their water-bearer crush is a mind reader, even though Aquarius certainly has many out-of-this-world qualities.

TAURUS & PISCES

Taurus sometimes fears that they lack imagination or that they're seen as boring—they've been told their whole life that they should be more flexible or try something new—so sometimes they can have a bit of a complex. Pisces also has their issues. Sometimes they feel that others don't believe in their abilities—they've been called flaky so many times that sometimes they start to believe other people's words! They both have pain, but when they come together, they heal each other and help one another grow. Pisces inspires Taurus's imagination, reminding them of how talented they are. Taurus's chill, grounded energy feels safe and supportive to Pisces, who finds a friend they can trust and count on in Taurus, and for whom they want to do the same.

These two are best friends and can be fantastic lovers, too. As a fling, they might flirt for quite a while before either of them makes a move, but when one of them does, it's powerful and intense. In the bedroom, Pisces's intuitive abilities meet Taurus's slow sensuality for a steamy lovemaking session filled with imagination and passion.

Long term, these two share an energetic home, busy with guests and dinner parties (although Taurus prefers it a bit quieter than Pisces does!). Taurus thinks Pisces is one of the coolest people they've ever met, while Pisces is fascinated by Taurus's mind.

GEMINI

THE TWINS

DATES: MAY 21–JUNE 21

PLANETARY RULER: MERCURY
ELEMENT: AIR
MODALITY: MUTABLE

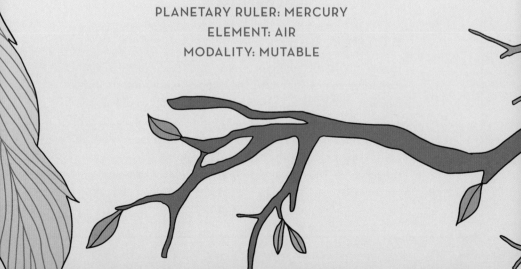

PERSONALITY

Two birds hop on a flowering tree branch in spring, chirping at each other, poking around curiously before taking off, looking down on the city and all its surroundings. Gemini, the sign of the twins, is an Air sign ruled by messenger planet Mercury. Contemplating duality, making choices, reflecting on either/or questions, coming to both/and conclusions—Gemini's mind is always busy.

Gemini can see all sides of a story, giving them the reputation of being "two-faced." However, if their wonderful ability to understand myriad points of view does manifest uncomfortably in relationships, it stems from a desire to keep things peaceful and moving, not out of malice.

Gemini is not just *in* the know, but a person *to* know, and it's a blessing indeed to be welcomed into their clique or crew. A media trendsetter, Gemini is a lover of all forms of news, both highbrow and low. Gemini is a prolific creator and rarely shies away from controversy, often whipping it up themself as they seek to challenge people's ideas about the world. Indeed, Gemini is one of the most controversial signs in the zodiac.

AT THEIR BEST

Highly intelligent, versatile, clever, and quick-witted, Gemini can adapt to any situation. Their good humor attracts many friends, and the twins rarely run out of things to talk about. They're fantastic wordsmiths, composers, idea makers, problem solvers, mediators, networkers, and trailblazers. Gemini cares very much about etiquette, and as controversial as they may be, they always strive to be polite. Understanding someone's point of view is important to them, and they value communication highly.

AT THEIR WORST

Their ability for multitasking can make them distracted and unfocused. These mercurial people can be tricksters or gossips, or they may speak cutting words. They play dumb from time to time, have been known to fib (Gemini? More like Gemi-lie!), and can be surprisingly superficial. Desperate to fit in, they can be envious, as well as territorial. They take everything literally *and* personally. They're nervous and can get lost in details and forget to look at the big picture. Being the "middleman" makes them stressed out. Emotional outbursts make them quite uncomfortable, and landing in a relationship where they find themself managing someone else's emotions is their personal nightmare. They believe everyone is an adult and should act like it, even though they can behave childishly at times.

LOVE PERSONALITY

A Gemini can break down any concept—but love? Even they know love is complicated—they've tried making sense of it, but haven't figured out the "trick" yet. But they're still very curious. The young Gemini falls in love and hopes they can make sense of this emotion. The mature Gemini falls in love and understands that, like all the other mysteries of life and death, love isn't something made for the human mind to comprehend.

Gemini is the sign of the twins, and as such, loves having a buddy to joke and have serious conversations with as well as explore the world. Gemini may have a reputation for being fickle; however, once they've met someone they really connect with, they can totally be committed partners. Once hard-to-pin-down Gemini initiates someone into their crew, they will remain solid friends. In fact, so solid that they're also known to recycle exes! Rarely does a Gemini do something (or someone!) once; *two* is their magic number.

Let's note that *committed* doesn't mean *rigid*, *boring*, or *inflexible*. As a mutable sign, none of those words is in their vocabulary, and open and polyamorous relationships are natural for many Gemini, a sign who values connecting with people. Other Gemini people prefer to be in a pair—but even so, their commitment won't be one that's suffocating or controlling.

FIRST IMPRESSIONS

Youthful, dashing, pixie-like, and often wearing glasses (to shield their eyes from the Sun after a long night out on the town, or for the more introverted of the twins, to help them read, as they're often doing), Gemini has a light, breezy energy. They're both exciting yet peaceful to be around. Even the quieter, more reserved Gemini has an upbeat spirit about them. You can usually guess that your new acquaintance is a Gemini by their stylish and cool vibe, easy ability to banter, familiarity with everyone in the neighborhood, and the smirk that seems to be planted on every twin's face.

Gemini is the sort of person who stands around with their arms folded, yet still seems open and inviting—there's a duality to this person that you can't miss. They're trendy in their fashions—whatever their clique is wearing, you'll likely see them in, too. They like clothes that are easy to run around in; the more versatile the piece, the better—they're masters of the day-to-night look.

FLIRTING TECHNIQUES

A matter-of-fact "I like you" works for logic-minded Gemini, a sign who's all about information, facts, and overthinking. Even the biggest Gemini players can wonder, *Wait—how does flirting work?*, when they meet someone they really like.

But once it's out there that you two are crushing on each other, body language is just as crucial as verbal affirmation (and yes, Gemini craves verbal affirmations and is typically very good at giving them, too). Nothing cheers Gemini up like a notification on their phone from someone they like. Balance dirty talk with sending nudes: a dirty video with well-manicured and clean nails (Gemini rules the hands) is usually appreciated.

"Negging" does not work with Geminis. They take things very literally, and being told something unkind by a stranger— or worse, a friend—is something they find uncomfortable at the very least.

Gemini loves a hustler, and a local celeb who has inside access to all the cool spots is certainly attractive to them. Being in the media is a plus, and while Gemini often goes after "cool" people, they are just as attracted to someone kind of nerdy, as they fall hard for smarts. They care that others carry themselves confidently and stylishly.

They appreciate the aloof types, as well as a cool approach to communication. However, they easily get bored with the "hard to catch" types, especially if they feel like someone is manipulating them by being unavailable. They prefer someone who is enthusiastic and involved with life and their community over someone who is jaded and can't have fun.

DATING STYLE

Gemini enjoys the courting process. They love a well-planned date, a thoughtful love letter, a surprising gift. An expensive date is always fun, and while they pretend candlelit dinners and flowers are cheesy, Gemini actually loves them. However, they're just as happy doing something cheap and easygoing—the amount of money you spend on Gemini doesn't matter to them as much as whether or not the experience is unique (bonus points if the venue is trendy or cool!).

Gemini is certainly spontaneous, but when it comes to dating, they do prefer to have things planned out—unless, of course, they're not serious about someone, in which case, they'll fit you into their schedule whenever they're in the mood to make out.

Local sights that make for scenic kisses and long strolls with fun conversation will make a Gemini's night. Gemini is social and enjoys being part of a scene, so a group date, swinging by a house party, or saying hi to friends at a regularly frequented café would be a fun, casual date that Gemini enjoys, in addition to the more romantic, private dates. Their top need is stimulating conversation. Have plenty of things to talk about and Gemini will go anywhere with you.

RELATIONSHIP APPROACH

Gemini craves variety, and while it's said that they get bored easily, this usually doesn't apply to the people in their lives—if there's one thing Gemini knows, it's that people are always changing and growing. Who Gemini is today isn't who they may be tomorrow, but they're excited to go on that journey with the people they care about.

Gemini sincerely wants to know about your day and wants you to care about theirs, too—so ask! As chatty as the twins are, they do appreciate having their own space, especially at home, where they might want to have at least one room to themself for their books, art, instruments, or whatever inspires them.

Communication is massively important to Gemini, and scheduling time together is crucial, too. Even though they are quite flexible, they want to know when they'll next hear from or see you. Gemini does get jealous, although they may be shocked when you act jealously. Understanding the people around them is incredibly important to them, and they expect the same from the people in their lives—Gemini will be hurt if you don't put the same effort into understating how they feel as they do for you.

The twins can get nervous quite easily, so if things get too stressful, they may dash in a hurry. Nervous Gemini jets when emotions become too overwhelming, but they'll usually reach out soon, at least once for closure. They are communicators, after all.

SEX

Curious Gemini is interested in all flavors, not just vanilla. Sex with the twins is never boring, and it's often kinky! They are eager to please and are excited to try new things. Visually driven, they respond best through your movements, but they also do love dirty talk. As the great communicator, they love hearing (and seeing) feedback. Spiritually, sexual climax allows them to connect more deeply with their body in a way that their very busy minds often prevent them from doing during everyday life.

Gemini loves nothing more than an innocent activity turning into something dirty. You're watching a movie together on the couch. A sex scene comes on, and you're both getting a little hot ... your hand brushes against their thigh. One thing leads to another, and movie night has just become something more!

TURN-ONS

Gemini is very visual. Being ruled by chatty Mercury, Gemini also loves dirty talk; however, they love watching what's happening just as much as they enjoy hearing you whisper things into their ear. During sex, touch each other in positions where Gemini can get a good view of what's happening.

Remember: Gemini is hot for cool people. Style is important to them, too, especially wearing something over the top, yet trendy, yet totally different from what the average person would dare to wear. It's a tall order, but you can do it! The pages of fashion magazines are littered with trends the average person wouldn't try—so find the sexiest, most cutting-edge one, and bring it into the bedroom!

Versatile in bed, they throw themself into sex very passionately, and their skilled hands are famous. What turns Gemini on is to turn *you* on. They can be quite romantic in bed, too, saying the sweetest things you could imagine, as well as the dirtiest. Let them know what you like in bed—they love the intellectual aspect of sharing what turns each of you on and then being able to do it together.

Gemini's versatility also means they're often switches, and they enjoy the intellectual side of kink—the academia, attending workshops, educating people on safety. The submissive Gemini can be quite childish or may enjoy feeling used or humiliated. The dominant Gemini will be much sterner than their usual, everyday playful personality, and will very much enjoy the psychological aspect of domination.

TURN-OFFS

Gemini doesn't have much patience for bad kissing; feeling as though they're just going through the motions in bed, as well as laziness, is a big turn-off.

Hygiene is very important! Bad breath, smelly sheets, or dirty fingernails are a no-no—take a shower!

Communication is very important to them, so don't expect them to be mind readers in bed. They don't *want* to guess what you desire, they want to hear you ask for it, and they want the praise when it's done well!

GEMINI & ARIES

There's no one cooler than fiery Aries in Gemini's eyes. Gemini doesn't see the hothead in Aries that many others do—they see someone straightforward, independent, and exciting. Aries, however, may find Gemini hard to pin down, which both excites and frustrates them—even the most available Gemini has a busy schedule that Aries must get used to. Once they're in the swing of things, these two can be best friends, as long as Gemini doesn't pull any trickster moves, which is sure to push Aries away. Aries needs to remember not to tease Gemini by alluding to the "cooler" friends they could be hanging out with—that would just hurt the twins' feelings (Hint: This is the *wrong* way for Aries to elicit attention!).

It's important that both signs remember to be themselves in this relationship. If Aries "tries something new" by going for a more mysterious, hard-to-catch vibe and not being their usual spontaneous, friendly selves, it will leave Gemini confused. And vice versa! If Gemini is trying to express themself differently after having been burned in the past by criticisms that they text too much or are too honest, Aries will be perplexed. One of the things Aries loves most about Gemini is their chatty nature. This is a tremendously fun, casual encounter, with both signs eager to outdo the other in passion and prowess, and long term, the spark stays alive thanks to Gemini's wit and imagination and Aries's ability to keep things fresh. Their home is cozy yet minimal. They both crave variation and new experiences, so they're sure to keep each other excited.

GEMINI & TAURUS

What you see is what you get with Taurus, but Gemini doesn't buy that. No, Gemini is very curious about Taurus and has plenty of questions for them. But they might also be a touch intimidated, too. There's something about Taurus that stirs deep, complicated feelings within Gemini. Taurus doesn't see what all the hubbub is about, but they're happy to answer all the many questions Gemini has (and Gemini has many). But Gemini isn't the only one who's a bit unsure. Taurus has their own insecurities. They see Gemini as someone who is so comfortable with change, movement, people, and communication, and Taurus wonders whether they have those skills, too. But Gemini would be wise to show their intellect and their emotional depth to Taurus, who has plenty to learn from Gemini. But Gemini must be careful not to act superficial, especially because Taurus gets turned off by a pompous attitude.

As much as Taurus loves to gossip and shop, they want to be with someone who is powerful, not petty. Taurus will need to do the same for Gemini, who craves intellectual stimulation. A way to Taurus's heart might be through their stomach, but Gemini's heart is found through their brain—they need smarts! Taurus adds luxurious touches to their home, while Gemini keeps things neat and orderly. The bedroom is emotionally intense, with both signs shedding insecurities and coming together despite their fears. Even as a fling, this union is powerful.

GEMINI & GEMINI

With both partners being Geminis, you would expect these two to have so much in common, but apart from their love of communication, it's rare that two Geminis will meet up at a time in their lives when they're both looking for and interested in the same thing—things are always changing for Gemini, you see. It doesn't matter, anyway. Gemini wants a partner who will excite and challenge them! They don't care so much about whether or not they have the same posse, but what they do care about is having a partner who can effortlessly join their group and expose their mind to new ideas while appreciating their way of doing things.

Friendship is important to both of them, but so is sex. Sex for two Geminis is a whirlwind of physical passion and mental connection—both are so critical to them. Their home is full of books, and they have useful gadgets everywhere. Geminis are often city people because they like to be where busy and interesting things are happening, but being close to nature—a hiking trail or a beach—is very good for their spirits, and they should encourage each other to connect with nature from time to time. When these two fight, it's brutal—while neither especially enjoys arguing, they still engage in it. When it does happen, both need to be mindful not to be mean or petty.

GEMINI & CANCER

Gemini isn't used to being called *mysterious*, so they're quite flattered when Cancer—someone Gemini thinks has their shit together—tells them they find them totally enigmatic. Of course, there's a chance that Cancer just thinks Gemini is a trickster who hides their true feelings and intentions for selfish reasons, or that Gemini thinks Cancer is greedy, selfish, and obsessed with cash. It all depends on the maturity level of these two. This relationship can work because both signs need their space and independence, and they both crave variety. However, they also covet feeling closeness with someone who will be part of their crew and their chosen family.

They share a sense of humor, which certainly helps build their relationship. The longer they spend building their friendship, the more fantastic memories they will have to share with one another, building an even stronger bond. Both Gemini and Cancer are sensitive creatures. Cancer expresses feelings in an obvious, emotional way, but Gemini worries internally. They often feel like they have to put on a happy face and keep people pleased, when in reality, Gemini wonders whether they're accepted by their peers.

Their home is thoughtfully curated, with Gemini organizing Cancer's clutter. Cancer loves their collections, and Gemini will love sorting through them, learning more about their partner through their interests and creating a space that's clean and airy. In bed, curious Gemini and nurturing Cancer get off on exploring their hidden desires—and they both have quite a few! For example, Gemini desires exploring kinks around power or even bondage, and Cancer is curious about everything from group sex to voyeurism or fantastical role-play!

GEMINI & LEO

These two best friends chat from morning to midnight—unless they hook up unexpectedly one day. Then there might be an awkward pause for about ninety minutes after they head home, until the texting resumes again. They have so much to talk about! And no, they don't just gossip and talk about superficial topics all day. They also talk about deep issues, like social justice, what's happening in their community, and the future of tech. These two signs love to have fun, but they also want to put their talents and resources to good use.

What about romance? Leo thinks Gemini is one of the most astonishing people they have ever met, and Leo, indeed, needs a partner who can live up to their standards. Gemini finds in Leo someone they can really connect with intellectually, which is truly what they are searching for. Gemini especially turns Leo on when they show how logically and reasonably they can approach a situation, and Leo would do well to reveal their wit.

These two are very busy and are unlikely to spend much time at home, but Gemini's sunny, airy, and well-organized home office is sure to have a different vibe from Leo's walk-in closet, which serves as so much more than a place for clothes and jewelry. It's also a hidden place to chat on the phone, to hide from the world, to cry, and—hey, there may even be a secret altar in there! The bedroom is full of excitement—Gemini is up for whatever Leo has in mind! With these two, there's sure to be long nights, both of them awake, chatting and sharing their hearts and their minds.

GEMINI & VIRGO

These two can be a little envious of each other, but this tension can be a turn-on and they're eager to take it into the bedroom. Both are ruled by the planet Mercury, which means they'll get to do what they love most: explore their curiosities. Gemini is very much a person Virgo admires—someone who inspires them creatively—and Gemini allows Virgo to explore their inventive side. Gemini, as nervous as they might be on the inside, is fantastic at talking with people—*schmoozing*, some would say—which is something shy Virgo has a hard time doing. But Gemini also admires Virgo for their ability to slow down, their intellect, their creativity, and their attention span. Yes, Virgo does get distracted, but they create supportive routines in their life, and that's something Gemini wants to learn from them.

Their energy in bed is a blend of Virgo's lusty, down-to-earth approach to lovemaking and Gemini's electric passion. This is a very hot one-night stand, and a friends-with-benefits situation could work out, as long as they maintain an open dialogue about their feelings and boundaries. Gemini needs a partner who is open-minded and free-spirited, so Virgo should be mindful about being judgmental or rigid too frequently around the Gemini they want to seduce. Virgo needs a partner who is imaginative and empathetic, so Gemini needs to practice listening skills. They can talk someone's ear off, but listening is a skill that they must develop. If they live together, the housewarming party will be one to remember, what with Gemini's contacts and Virgo's party-planning skills.

GEMINI & LIBRA

Gemini had a crush on Libra the moment they walked into the room. Libra is used to this kind of attention, but Gemini? They're not used to falling so hard just on someone's vibe. You see, they're both Air signs, so they both deeply crave intellectual connection. Brains are important to them, and just as crucial as the heart.

And for their hearts to beat for each other, Gemini finds creative inspiration through Libra, although no sign should be referred to as a *muse*; Libra isn't into being objectified. But Libra is deeply turned on by Gemini's mind and loves to listen to their stories about their travels, dreams, goals, and philosophies. If they want to win each other's hearts even more, Gemini would be wise

to show what a loyal friend they are and that they stick up for the people they care about. Libra, the diplomat, should also reveal their competitive side because no one wins a debate like Libra, and it definitely turns Gemini on.

And what are their turn-ons in bed? Libra is glad to find that Gemini is curious to explore their fantasies, and Gemini, who is so visual, will adore Libra's sexy presence in the bedroom. Communication is important to them, but they need to make sure to spend time with each other, not with their phones, when they go out on a date. If they live together, having a shared social life, as well as their own friendships, will give them both the community they crave and the space they need.

GEMINI & SCORPIO

Everyone thinks Scorpio is so intense—except Gemini, who sees the more grounded and strategic side of Scorpio. Gemini sees the aspect of Scorpio that's ready to sit down and do the *hard stuff* of getting things *done*, of creating a productive and fruitful life, and of working through trauma. Yes, all these things are intense, but Gemini doesn't see it as overwhelming; they see it as power. And Scorpio rather likes being seen that way! Scorpio sees great depth in Gemini as well, despite the fact that this is a sign who is often accused of being shallow or superficial. Yes, Gemini can totally be surface level sometimes, but that doesn't mean that they don't have deep feelings. And Scorpio is capable of sitting with them through difficult matters. They can make great transformations together as a couple.

A friends-with-benefits situation or even a one-night stand is sure to be intense, but they have different ways of corresponding, so they need to be patient with each other as they figure out how best to communicate with one another. In bed, the energy is incredibly passionate. Gemini's adaptability means they can fit into whatever wild scene Scorpio dreams up—and the scorpion will dream up many wild scenes. If they decide to live together, social butterfly Gemini would be wise to spend a few nights in with Scorpio, snuggling on the couch, and Scorpio should plan some fun adventurous weekends for the two of them to go on.

GEMINI & SAGITTARIUS

They feel at home with each other, which is funny, because *home* is something that's a little bit of a mystery to them both. You see, growing up for Sagittarius, home was a disorganized, messy, and emotionally charged place, and for Gemini, it was quite sterile and too "perfect," making it hard to unwind. Gemini dreamed of running away—even if things weren't *bad* per se at home. Gemini is an adventurer who has always felt ready to be off seeing the world on their own. Even from a young age, they spent time away, gallivanting with friends. Sagittarius wanted to run away, too—or perhaps a better way to phrase it, run free—to explore the world, see all the sights, learn as much as possible, and spread their own ideas, as well.

These two signs are both curious and intelligent and love to connect with others—no wonder they feel so comfortable with each other! They both give each other the space they need to do their own thing, and they're never disappointed when they come together to share stories about their adventures. Together, these two explorers will share and partake in many escapades together. Their sexual energy is exciting and electric. If they choose to keep their relationship as a fantastic fling, they'll most likely hook up periodically throughout the years, but if they both want to commit, they will be able to withstand even a long distance. If they live together, their home will be filled with souvenirs from their travels, as well as plenty of space to get work done.

GEMINI & CAPRICORN

Gemini is ruled by Mercury, a planet that is all about data, and Capricorn is ruled by Saturn, a planet that appreciates facts. Does this sound romantic? Maybe not, but as either of these signs can tell you, a relationship built on a solid foundation with healthy boundaries, a respect for each other's time, and a regard for the truth is the best kind there is. Whether it's a casual fling or a long-term thing, these two will learn a lot from loving (and adjusting to) each other. Most Geminis are very thoughtful and value honesty and communication, and Capricorns are eager to build a home with a supportive, loving person in their life.

Gemini would be wise to display their nurturing abilities to Capricorn—everything from the mundane, like cooking for them, to the emotional, such as being present with Capricorn during difficult times. Capricorn loves to complain—it's an Earth sign thing—but they would be wise not to smother Gemini with negativity. Complaining is a pastime to Capricorn, but a stressor to Gemini. But Capricorn is also extremely proactive and takes initiative to fix things, too.

In the bedroom, Capricorn's down-to-earth sensuality and big collection of kinky bedroom accessories excites curious and versatile Gemini. If they live together, Gemini can help Capricorn stay healthy and moving instead of always sitting at their desk, perhaps by inspiring them to go on walks around the neighborhood together. In return, Capricorn should encourage Gemini to practice mindfulness and retreat from their busy intellect by building them a space in which to meditate. This meditation room is sure to be a silk hammock for "aerial yoga," allowing Gemini to show off their acrobatics (in more ways than one). Capricorn loves *any* purchase that turns out to be widely useful, and indeed, Gemini, the sign of the twins, can show them many ways to work with anything!

GEMINI & AQUARIUS

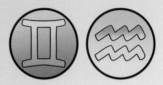

Aquarius takes Gemini on the adventures they long to go on, and Gemini invites Aquarius to the parties they've always wanted to be invited to. Aquarius is totally inspired by Gemini's creativity and their exuberance for life, while Gemini is in awe of Aquarius's brilliant mind.

They get along so well! Well, usually, that is. Aquarius is a *fixed* sign, which means they can be quite stubborn, something Gemini will either adore and lean on or be completely frustrated by. Gemini is a *mutable* sign, flexible and adaptable, busy and social. Aquarius is social, too—but not to the extent Gemini is. They may feel left out when Gemini goes out to play, even though Gemini most likely invited them and Aquarius said no of their own

accord. If they want this to be more than a fling, then Gemini would be wise to show their loyalty and dependability, and Aquarius should go on some of the adventures Gemini suggests, instead of being the only one to plan the dates.

Their energy in the bedroom is electric! Their ease communicating with one another means that these two will have plenty of fun between the sheets. Verbal affirmation is important to them both, so keeping the lines of communication open is crucial. But they don't only chat with each other frequently; they're also connected to plenty of other people, so when they're home together, it would be wise to schedule screen-free time so they can give each other their undivided attention.

GEMINI & PISCES

Their landscapes are so different for Gemini and Pisces—the fish swims in the deep, vast ocean, while the twins play on dry land. But the grass (or seaweed) is often greener on the other side. Who among us hasn't wondered what it would be like to live underwater, and of course, we're all familiar with the Hans Christian Andersen story of the Little Mermaid, who longed to be on land. Water is the realm of emotion, while Air is the dominion of intellect—these two can team up to be a couple that listens empathetically but also offers constructive help.

It's not just Pisces who lends their psychic and sympathetic ear to Gemini, but Gemini also holds space for Pisces—you see, Pisces feels very at home with Gemini. And Pisces offers Gemini constructive, logical insight, as Gemini looks up to Pisces creatively; Gemini is very attracted to Pisces's imagination and intuitive abilities.

Meanwhile, Gemini's cool, logical approach is very attractive to Pisces—as long as Gemini is open to Pisces's mystical ways. If Gemini looks down on any of Pisces's superstitious trinkets (their good luck seashell or their lucky penny), then Pisces will feel misunderstood by Gemini. Pisces's artistic qualities are very attractive to Gemini, but Pisces would be wise to make efforts not to wallow in self-pity and to be proactive about conquering their goals—Gemini wants to be with someone who is motivated and optimistic.

They're both very versatile in the bedroom. Pisces's romantic energy mingled with Gemini's curiosity makes for plenty of fun and sweet kisses between the sheets. Even if it's just a short fling, these two will learn a lot from each other in a short amount of time. If they decide to live together, this learning will continue for as long as they're partners—perfect for a pair that's so curious.

CANCER

THE CRAB

DATES: JUNE 21–JULY 22

PLANETARY RULER: THE MOON
ELEMENT: WATER
MODALITY: CARDINAL

PERSONALITY

Waves crash—a powerful rush, followed by the ocean gently pulling back—on the shore where the crab calls home. Home is an important theme to Cancer. Their crab shell is symbolic of their journey toward developing a life that is safe, protected, and sturdy, capable of deflecting the bullshit life tosses at them and holding them while things are running smoothly.

Ruled by the Moon, a symbol for the womb, Cancer is extremely affectionate and caring, and just like Luna's shape shifts day by day, Cancer too has many sides: sometimes they are full, dramatically shining brightly for all to see, and sometimes they retreat to the dark, to cool off and spend time in solitary reflection.

It is the first Water sign on the zodiac wheel and a cardinal sign, making Cancer the first sign of its season, which in this case is summer. Psychically and emotionally sensitive, this Water sign expresses their cardinality through their tenacity and ability to shield, hold, and protect.

AT THEIR BEST

Protective and nurturing, the crab is a superb listener, a caring friend, and a devoted lover who will treat you like family. They are tenacious, and despite their sometimes shy disposition, they bravely fight to achieve success in whatever field they are passionate about. Their homes are havens of peace and harmony, where you can always have a cup of hot tea on a cozy couch. They have profound emotional depth, making the crab feel deeply and highly intuitive.

AT THEIR WORST

Moody and defensive, the crab can jump to conclusions. They expect total understanding from everyone around them, and assume others to be mind readers. As nurturing and protective as they can be, they can also lie, cheat, and be sneaky. There is a dark side to the Moon, and these crustaceans can be full of shit. They can be very clingy—those crab claws have some real pinching power. But these crustaceans can easily become ghost crabs. Small and cowardly, they can be too wimpy to resolve an issue, choosing to retreat rather than deal with confrontation, which is in sharp contrast to their bold ability to start drama.

LOVE PERSONALITY

Cancer's ultimate destiny is to create a safe and nurturing home. Finding the right person to do it with is the big question, but one Cancer isn't necessarily looking to answer right away. Scuttling around the beach in their protective shell, Cancer dances from side to side. The crab meets many people during their life's journey, and they're not in a total rush to settle down, because when they do, they want it to *work*. They are the first sign of summer, making them a cardinal sign, but unlike cardinal Aries, who is the first sign of spring, Cancer is not impulsive.

Whether it's the family they were born into or the one they choose for themself, family is very important to Cancer. A Cancer in love treats their partner with the same respect, care, humor, tenderness, and honesty that they would with their family, and they expect the same in return.

Their disposition can swing, but if you're in sync with them, it's something you'll learn to accept and get used to. They may be quiet all day, and then burst into chatter at night after the lights have been turned off—sharing a funny joke while holding you in bed. Or your crab lover may have been playful and in a creative zone all day before becoming more reserved or emotional later on.

FIRST IMPRESSIONS

Because Cancer is ruled by the always changing Moon, your first impression of the crab will probably depend on what day it is. Sometimes more outgoing, other times more reserved, they can be wacky and playful one moment and then serious and focused the next. They can be the coldest or kindest person you have ever met. That said, they will always exude a protective aura around themself and their loved ones.

Even the most scientifically minded Cancer is intuitive and highly creative. Cancers are typically fashionable, and even if they don't care for clothes, they often run with people who do. It's not unusual to meet a crab whose outfit consists of a vintage piece from abroad, a designer piece from an ex, and a hand-knit item from their mom.

On that note, have you noticed I haven't mentioned *mom* at all in Cancer's chapter? Cancer's so-called obsession with their momma is an overdone trope, but *mother* is an important part of Cancer's life—or at least an important aspect of the archetype of this sign. Understanding their relationship, or lack of relationship, with their mother is important to understanding them.

FLIRTING TECHNIQUES

True to the crab's side-to-side shuffle, they don't like confrontation. Sure, they have their bold moments when they'll boisterously ask you out, but they may become shy the next time you see them. Generally, they like a slow buildup to occur between themself and those they have set their sights on. Not only does it give them a chance to make sure that the object of their affection is cool, sane, and sexy, but the anticipation is also a turn-on for them.

It's okay to be a bit aloof and reserved with your crab. They might be shy, but they genuinely love the chase and are surprisingly dominant, considering the homemaker reputation they've developed by being so sweet. They are attracted to hard workers who are reliable and practical and have lived full lives brimming with excitement and joy after overcoming hardships. A dry sense of humor doesn't hurt! And having a secret naughty side is especially enticing.

If you missed your chance to flirt with a Cancer in the past, don't worry! You'll likely get your shot again if you run into them some other time. They're very nostalgic—even if it's only been six months since you've seen them, they'll want to know if you still talk to so-and-so or still visit the same places, giving you an opportunity to ask for the date you hadn't been able to propose before!

They might *think* they are picky, but once they fall in love (or lust) with someone, it will usually be because of how they made them *feel*, not totally because of how they look; however, style is certainly very important to them: a polished, grown-up, tailored look is likely to do the trick.

DATING STYLE

Even the flashiest Cancer has a very frugal side, and often they would rather go to a market with their date, buy some groceries, and cook at home together than go out to a restaurant for dinner. This is also in alignment with their homebody selves. Cancers love their homes, so spend time with them at their place. A beautiful breakfast the morning after a date is a key romantic gesture for Cancer, likely even more important than the date itself!

But sweet, homemaker Cancer has a surprising side to their personality. They love the occult, and they're not afraid of graveyards. Ask them to go someplace a bit scary—maybe a walk through the local cemetery or by a so-called haunted house. Bonus points if it's a rainy day, so you can snuggle under the umbrella. They also love sex and won't shy away from a sex party, so if one comes up, invite your partner!

If you are dating the rare Cancer who is freaked out by either suggestion (anything is possible with the changeable crab!), carving out quality time for a heart-to-heart talk about the past, the future, and all your feelings is never a bad idea. Have a box of tissues close by in case one of you starts crying.

RELATIONSHIP APPROACH

Moody Cancer needs a lot of personal space, but then again, they really need you to be there. I would tell you it all depends on the Moon, but I don't want to remove your responsibility to communicate with them or their responsibility to communicate with you. Never blame boundary issues on astrology!

Cancers are very cautious about who they settle down with. Family is important to them, and whomever they settle down with will need to fit in. You need to prove yourself—mostly that you're not a hasty idiot who blindly falls into trouble. Cancers need security. They also need to be with someone who has a dark sense of humor and knows how to have a good time—without anyone getting into trouble with the police, or at least getting caught.

Whether the crab is in a polyamorous or a monogamous relationship, it is crucial to them that they don't feel used, and that the energy they put forth is appreciated.

If you have your sights set on a Cancer, there could still be an ex or a friend with benefits hanging around. Between their heavy nostalgia and their sometimes phobia of cleanly breaking things off with people, this can be an issue. But not always! Maturity level is obviously a factor here, so check in with yourself and your partner. Have an honest discussion about your boundaries and your needs so they can decide whether or not they want to say goodbye to the past to pursue a future with you . . . and, hey, if you do "move on" and end the relationship, realize that *you* might now become the "old love" they are nostalgic for!

SEX

Cancers may appear shy, but don't be fooled. They very much enjoy pursuing their crushes and like to take charge in relationships. Cancer may be the homemaker of the zodiac, but they are incredibly freaky. They're intrigued by power and domination in bed, so ask them how they feel about BDSM.

Don't be afraid to queef, fart, sweat, squirt, or slurp around them. These things don't turn them on per se, but something about the messy side of sex just makes them feel giddy. If something is noisy, wet, and messy, Cancer thinks it's a good time.

Highly emotional people, Cancers find sex to be a deeply transformative act. It's a physical expression of love that not only brings them closer to their lover, but also helps them process the many complicated feelings they experience. It's a chance to relax, tune out the outside world, and connect with their partner (or with themself through masturbation), which is an important experience for them.

TURN-ONS

Big boobs, little boobs, perky butts, giant butts, pecs and calves, peach fuzz and hairy patches are all good! The crab loves bodies and everything about them. Smother them with your body and they'll likely be into it.

Crabs have a fantastic imagination, and this translates to the bedroom as well. Get whimsical! Whether it's a vampire snacking on its prey's blood or runaways who have joined the circus and are cuddling together on a cold night on the road, Cancers get a thrill out of role-play, and on exploring power dynamics, too, so bust out the sexy disciplinary attitude.

Submissive Cancers enjoy being teased—both in the sense of being humiliated as well as orgasm control. Dominant Cancers enjoy rope bondage and handcuffs as well as 24/7 lifestyles—think, a collar around the neck at dinnertime. Invoke their crab claws by experimenting with nipple clamps, and while you are at the sex toy shop, pick up some restraints and lube (the wetter the better!). Kinky Cancer is up for nearly anything!

Sex on the beach is not just a drink but an act that this Water sign would enjoy. They often feel at home by the water, and we all know how much Cancer values their home life. The body parts associated with the crab are the chest, breasts, and stomach, so caress them tenderly and kiss them on these spots.

TURN-OFFS

Passionate make-up sex is fine with the crab, but if you pick a new fight while you're under the sheets, don't expect it to ramp up the energy. Cautious Cancer will get defensive during intimate moments.

Cancers are touchy, unless it's during a consensual scene, so don't criticize them, even playfully, if you're hoping to have sex soon. "You look a little bloated" is definitely not an opening line to lead with!

CANCER & ARIES

Prudent Cancer is strategic with the use of their pincers, but spontaneous Aries head butts their way through problems. From a distance, this is exciting to Cancer, but if they're going to be in a long-term relationship and not just a short fling, Aries needs to realize that their impulsivity is jarring to Cancer. But if they decide to keep it short, these two will have a very passionate and fun time.

Cancer looks up to Aries for their bravery, their ability to put themself out there, and their passion for success. With Cancer, Aries is able to create a home, to learn about making a safe space for themself. They inspire and support each other like no one else can—but that doesn't mean they don't have their differences. Aries needs to slow down, and Cancer needs to be more straightforward.

Cancer is an amazing listener, which is one of Aries's favorite aspects about them. To attract an Aries, the Cancer would be wise to show how well they get along with others—their nurturing ability is very attractive to Aries. As for Aries, they may need to put in more work. They need to prove to Cancer that they can be responsible and reliable, which totally depends on the maturity level of the ram.

Protection is a theme closely tied to Cancer, so why not team up with Aries, a sign who's also eager to defend and fight for those they love? Aries would be very appreciative of Cancer's tender, nurturing touch like no other. This can be a fairy-tale romance, with both characters saving each other.

CANCER & TAURUS

There are two ways to get Taurus to be more flexible about things: make them think it was their idea during a shopping trip, or make them food that they can eat while you implant a suggestion. Cancer is talented in the kitchen and can be persuasive when necessary, so they'll be able to get Taurus to open up to all sorts of things! No one can get a Taurus to change their mind like a Cancer can, and honestly, there's no one cooler Cancer could imagine being with. Cancer loves art and culture, but Taurus is connected to the scene in a way that Cancer admires and wants to be a part of.

These two are the best of friends—talking all day and being patient with one another's faults. Frugal Cancer is so excited to be able to dig through Taurus's closet and borrow all of their designer clothes, and Taurus is totally happy to lend them a few pieces in exchange for a cup of tea and an ear to listen to them as they express their worries.

Their home is a fantastic place to host parties, with Taurus adding an opulent touch and Cancer adding the heart needed to make a house a home. On the off chance their energies don't align, it may be because Taurus is being snobby or Cancer is being impossible to reach out to, but generally this pair has the patience to make a relationship work.

Their energy in the bedroom is romantic and sensual, and they have the communication flow to discuss what they crave easily. Cancer shouldn't be nervous to be over-the-top sexy with Taurus, and Taurus should feel comfortable expressing their boundaries to Cancer—Cancer loves a partner who knows what they want. And Taurus, indeed, knows what they want... unless, of course, Cancer works their magic and changes the bull's mind.

CANCER & GEMINI

Cancer sees Gemini as a mystery, which is funny because Gemini is happy to tell you what's on their mind. Gemini is always busy moving around, asking questions about the world, and figuring things out. To them, Cancer seems to have gotten it all together, which is something they'll either admire or feel intimidated by. Cancer needs to show their adventurous side if they want to win Gemini over, while Gemini is going to need to prove that they can be serious—at least as often as they can be a trickster.

Together, they share a fantastic sense of humor, which will get them through most bumps in the road, but they'll need to be careful about telling each other little white lies just to keep the peace. They need to remember that an honest and open conversation will be more constructive for them in the long run. Cancer's not going to put up with any shady answers from Gemini—and Gemini's not going to put up with any moody behavior, either.

They both share a wacky side, enjoying visiting carnivals, sideshows, and flea markets. But as much as they enjoy exploring the weird side of life, these two value their home life even more, including spending time in their neighborhoods, often sharing a favorite coffee shop or restaurant. In bed, the energy is exciting, as they find new things to reveal to and teach each other whenever they hook up. At home, Gemini is a minimalist, but Cancer will make sure there are some beautiful touches here and there.

CANCER & CANCER

Cautious Cancer walks from side to side, waiting for the perfect time to pinch. Neither of these two is very direct about what they want, but they manage to get their heart's desire anyway! They're both tenacious people, and not just when it comes to their professional goals. If they love someone, they'll do whatever they can to make things work.

Can these two crabs be in a relationship? Of course! They'll respect each other's need for space, while also giving one another plenty of emotional support, spending time and energy to help each other process complicated emotions. They're both very nostalgic, and late-night talks about the past and complications they've endured are sure to come up. They just need to be careful not to guilt trip, play games, or pout about their partner not being a strong enough mind reader about their problems. Life can be so unpredictable—but Cancers can win each other over by showing how consistently responsive and responsible they are with each other's needs and emotions.

They can amass great wealth together—but they need to be careful not to start collecting and hoarding lots of crap. Their home is where they are able to recharge and regain balance, so it is a very important place for them. In the bedroom they're both very raunchy, which makes for fantastic chemistry. These two signs are very empathetic and emotional, which are some of their best qualities, but they'll have to remember to show their cool and rational side if they want things to work out for more than just a cozy weekend cuddle-up.

CANCER & LEO

The luminaries: Leo is the Sun, Cancer is the Moon. One might dominate the night sky, and the other the day, but these two can certainly share a scene. Let's take a moment to reflect on these luminaries and where they stand. Leo is used to being the center of attention. Yes, the Moon spins around the Sun, but the primary orbit of the Moon is around the Earth. Leo doesn't know what to make of someone who has a primary focus other than them! But that makes Cancer all the more enticing to Leo, a big cat that's happy to have a new mouse to chase.

Cancer looks at Leo and sees someone who is confident, self-assured, and decked in jewels—and it might inspire some insecurity in them. Leo looks at Cancer and . . . has no idea what to make of them! Cancer is a total mystery to Leo, and mystery spells drama for Leo—their magic key word. They have a lot of complicated emotions to work out with each other, which will make this coupling interesting. Cancer needs to open up to Leo and understand that being secretive will confuse their lion lover, and Leo needs to be patient with the crab, who needs to do things at their own pace.

Their home will be a combination of Leo's dramatic touches and Cancer's nurturing energy. The energy in bed is very emotional and passionate. Leo feels a little insecure around Cancer, unsure whether or not Cancer's focus is really on Leo, but once a good rapport is built, and if Leo is able to get over some of their paranoia about Cancer, these two can be a power couple, stealing attention everywhere they go.

CANCER & VIRGO

These two aren't just best friends because Cancer likes having someone who will clean up after they cook, but because communication between the two of them just works—Virgo is logical and yet intuitive, something Cancer really appreciates in a partner. Virgo is inspired by Cancer's nurturing abilities and also simply thinks they have excellent taste—Virgo enjoys seeing what kind of art Cancer will come home with next or what vacation road trip idea they might come up with. Not only that, but Virgo also enjoys meeting Cancer's friends and being part of their community.

These two can talk about anything, from their emotions to their business strategy—they may even choose to work together. Virgo always has a few projects they're excited about doing, and Cancer loves helping take the lead on any kind of moneymaking scheme.

Cancer's moodiness can come across as very icy to Virgo, and Virgo's nitpickyness is sure to hurt Cancer's feelings on more than one occasion. Virgo might find that they'll "win" all the arguments by being right . . . but being right might not be worth getting the silent treatment from Cancer, a sign who needs their space while they process for a few days (or weeks!).

If they stay together as more than a fling (and these two can easily be friends with benefits), their home will be filled with knickknacks they've found along their journeys. The energy in bed is a blend of Virgo's curiosity and sensuality and Cancer's intuitive touch.

CANCER & LIBRA

They're both looking for something very different than what the other typically has to offer; however, when they both think the other is hot, what are they going to do?

Cancer is usually most attracted to people who are very realistic, practical, and grounded. And while Libra can certainly be these things, it's not what you'll first notice about them. Cancer would be wise to get to know Libra beyond their stylish demeanor. Cancer might be cautious, but that doesn't mean they don't make snap decisions about people.

When Cancer gets to know Libra, they'll be surprised by how at home they feel with them. Libra is searching for a partner who is strong, confident, straightforward, and fiery—they're looking for a spark. Cancer's cautious, sometimes moody, demeanor isn't what Libra expects to fall in love with either, but once they get to know the crab better, they find that Cancer is someone nurturing and protective, which they love. Cancer, too, helps push Libra toward their professional goals, and Libra can always use a cheerleader.

There's a side to Libra that can be a little vain, and indeed, Cancer is certainly someone they love having on their arm at parties. Their home is filled with antiques and beautiful objects, and their bedroom is a soothing place where they can retreat to forget about their day and enjoy each other's company. Their sexual energy is magnetic and also filled with a degree of tension, so sparks fly in the bedroom.

CANCER & SCORPIO

Cancer may be a homemaker, but it is their travels around the world, their intelligence, and their faith that attract Scorpio to them—not to mention the intense chemistry these two Water signs feel for one another.

Scorpio might be one of the most mysterious signs in the zodiac, but Cancer sees the side of them that is full of spirit, loves to celebrate life, and enjoys being creative. There's an ease between these two signs; however, they're both a little suspicious of things that are too simple, or too easy, and they may stir up some drama just to prove to themselves that there is depth and real feelings, and that their relationship is not fake or superficial.

They do have their issues. Scorpio gets upset when they feel like Cancer is trying to outsmart them, and Cancer gets overwhelmed by Scorpio's self-destructive tendencies. Cancer needs to be careful not to be too hot and cold with their Scorpio love, because Scorpio really needs consistency from their partners. Scorpio needs to learn that the Moon, Cancer's ruler, has its phases. Scorpio would be wise to show their responsible side to Cancer—it turns them on, almost as much as Scorpio's open-mindedness in the bedroom! Their sexual chemistry is fantastic. They have a special connection in bed, and they consistently find ways to explore one another. Yes, these two are very emotional; however, it's the adventure in the bedroom that delights them.

CANCER & SAGITTARIUS

Whether it's a fling or something long-term, these two find each other making big changes in their lives as a result of the other's influence. Sagittarius is an adventurer—and the journey they go on when they're with Cancer is one of transformation, letting go of the past (all travelers know that too much baggage is a drag), and learning how to open up and deeply connect with someone else. Nostalgic Cancer has some letting go of the past to do, too, so this is something they can heal together.

Cancer resists outside help or the idea that they need to get organized, get healthy, and create a routine. But with Sag, they're able to find a groove that allows them to be more produc-tive. It's likely they'll break a bad habit or two with Sagittarius around—either by Sag being a good influence, or by watching Sag overindulge and deciding that kind of life is not for them!

Sagittarius says things Cancer wouldn't dream of blurting out—but that's often why Cancer is drawn to Sag! And Sagittarius is mesmerized by Cancer's creative abilities—as an artist, chef, businessperson, or whatever it may be. Their home is their oasis from the outside world, and their bedroom is filled with memories of long, long nights of lovemaking. Sagittarius's fire combined with Cancer's imagination is a recipe for total pleasure. Sagittar-ius loves it when Cancer is in one of their chattier moods, and these two can have the most fun late at night talking about their past selves. Cancer is inspired by Sagittarius's speeches about right and wrong—something Sag has plenty of opinions about!

CANCER & CAPRICORN

On paper, Capricorn's got what Cancer wants in a person: stability, a drive for success, and a love of sex. And the feeling is mutual. Capricorn craves intimacy and closeness, a person they can find home with, and someone protective and nurturing. Although it's true that Capricorn can be very chilly when you first meet them, they take their relationships seriously—like they take everything—and need depth from their partners. But *both* of these signs know that what someone is on paper means nothing until they prove themself, and this takes time . . . and time is a concept that's deeply embedded in these two signs' energies, Capricorn being ruled by Saturn, the planet of time, and Cancer being ruled by the Moon, one of humans' oldest calendar devices.

Careful Cancer is willing to wait and see what time tells them, and so is patient Capricorn. But the goat is also very busy and isn't going to stand for any wishy-washy behavior on Cancer's part. As for Capricorn, they will need to watch out about poking too much fun at their crabby friend. Although Cancer may appear to have a tough shell, if they let you in, you better respect their softness and not make fun of them!

Together, Cancer and Capricorn can build a beautiful home with a lasting legacy, preserving old traditions and starting new ones together. On the outside, this couple might seem strait-laced, but they really let loose in the bedroom. Expect to find a trunk full of toys under their luxury mattress—these two signs are smart with cash but don't like to skimp where it counts, and the bedroom is certainly a place of high value to them.

CANCER & AQUARIUS

Cool Aquarius and moody Cancer are really quite kooky when they come together—it's a pleasant surprise for all involved! Yes, things can be awkward, especially at first. There will be a lot of learning experiences and growing pains, and they'll need to work on breaking bad habits, as well as opening up more deeply in a relationship than they previously may have been used to.

Aquarius sometimes feels like they need to map out their emotions, to create an equation to help them understand their feelings—like, *no food plus bad traffic equals bad temper*—while Cancer laughs at the idea that feelings could be broken down so easily. Yes, these two have plenty of math and psychology classes to put each other through, with Aquarius trying to add things up while Cancer pulls out the couch for the water bearer to recline

on as the crab takes notes during their psychoanalysis.

What keeps them going is their shared sense of humor. Cancer shouldn't be afraid of being a show-off around Aquarius, who loves a partner who isn't afraid to be proud of their talents. Aquarius is known to be the rebel of the zodiac, but they're still a reliable friend and partner, and to woo the conscientious crab, the water bearer will need to display this side to Cancer.

As a fling, they're sure to have a wild time, and long term, their home will be filled with DIY trinkets and homemade devices they welded together some night at 3 a.m. when neither of them could sleep. In the bedroom, Aquarius is thrilled by Cancer's imagination, while Cancer is turned on by Aquarius's cool mystique.

CANCER & PISCES

As the last sign on the zodiac wheel, Pisces has seen a lot of shit—and Cancer is eager to hear all about it. Remember, Cancer longs to have a partner who's lived a full life. Pisces is interested in the crab, too! They think Cancer is so fun and creative, they just want to be around the crab's glow. These two Water signs come together easily, but can it last? A fling between these two is sure to be a good time; however, they *both* can get very annoyed by the other's seemingly laissez-faire attitude.

Pisces is used to being accused of being too unreliable a partner, but when the fish meets Cancer, they meet someone who (often unintentionally) is even busier doing their own thing. Cancer is always having fun and sometimes will have an invitation without Pisces's

name on it. These two Water signs will both need to be mindful of *including* one another. If they can do that and get into a regular routine with each other, this can be an amazing combination.

These two excite and inspire each other every day. Cancer enjoys listening to Pisces's musings on their life and their thoughts about the world, and Pisces feels nurtured by Cancer's touch. Their home has an airy vibe, but the bedroom is quite intense—deep emotions are explored and ecstatic heights are reached, as these two signs aren't afraid to "go there" and explore any fantasy or feeling—and so is the bathroom, especially when these two get into the shower together! Two Water signs in a tub means things are sure to get steamy.

LEO

THE LION

DATES: JULY 22–AUGUST 23

PLANETARY RULER: THE SUN
ELEMENT: FIRE
MODALITY: FIXED

PERSONALITY

A fire blazes. People sit around, roasting marshmallows, telling stories, staying warm. Food, friendship, comfort. It all happens around the fire, and like a blazing fire, Leo loves to be the warmth that radiates out to all their loved ones, bringing them joy and nourishment, just like the life-giving Sun does for us on Earth. And like the Sun, Leo is at the center of life's parties and pleasures.

Fire sign Leo is ruled by the Sun—a symbol of life and vitality. As a fixed sign, Leo falls in the middle of the season—summer in this case—making this Sun reliable, consistent, and sometimes a little too hot, like its ruling planet. This determined, gregarious, and regal lion was born to do great things and enjoys being a beacon of positivity for their community, but, like a fire in a hearth, if no one is there to benefit from their warmth, what's it all for? A leader and a performer, confident Leo is most of all a lover.

AT THEIR BEST

Creatives with a heart of gold, these brave and loyal lions care deeply about the joy and comfort of the people around them. Fantastic leaders, mentors, teachers, and coaches, outgoing and ambitious Leo also knows how to party, creating a fun and celebratory environment wherever they go. They have a regal energy about them. Being onstage comes naturally to them, and their confidence is infectious—their smile is genuine and heartwarming. Reliable, optimistic, trusting of their own instincts, and bighearted, Leo is an exciting, irreplaceable person to have in your life.

AT THEIR WORST

Leo is known for their confident nature, but sometimes their attitude can go too far and align more with shameless egomania, assuming the world revolves around them. They can lose their cool when people don't kiss their ass because they're quite sure they're better than everyone else. Very sensitive to criticism, they can dish it, but they can't always take it and can resort to belittling those around them. Desperate to fit in, these arrogant and possessive people aren't strangers to temper tantrums. Did I mention stubborn, vain, and self-absorbed? Rose-colored glasses? These big cats are perpetually gazing into a rose-colored mirror.

LOVE PERSONALITY

How can you not take love seriously when you're the sign that rules the heart? Love is the meaning of life for Leo. Without love, what's the point? With a flair for the dramatic, Leo loves productions and theatrics. A relationship that's punctuated with excitement certainly keeps the spark alive, but of course there is more to Leo than that: Leo is looking for their equal in loyalty.

Leo's love is protective and nurturing, eager to heal and grow their heart with yours. Just like a lion, Leo's pack is important to them. Leo is a responsible and reliable partner, and they're attracted to people who are as considerate as they are but who have unexpected or unique qualities—Leo wants a partner who is unlike anyone else in the world!

Leo knows that the more love there is in the world, the better place it will be. And despite their love of theatrics, when they make a promise, you can be sure they'll hold it close to their heart.

FIRST IMPRESSIONS

Leo has a big presence. Whether they're rocking big hair (or a beard) and big sunglasses or wearing something flashy, they have the aura of a celebrity, and when you first meet them, you are starstruck. They are confident, and even though they exude such power and poise, they're usually very warm and friendly, too. Ruled by the Sun, Leo is a sunny person, indeed. Their star power makes them hard to miss, and they don't even need to be intoxicated for them to be convinced to dance on a table at a nightclub. They're the ones singing the most ambitious song at karaoke. But they never embarrass themself. This big cat is too regal and poised!

If you meet them online, you'll notice their photos are usually of them at a party, surrounded by friends, traveling someplace exotic, or posing with some over-the-top prop. Or maybe it's a "behind the scenes" image of them at the gym or trying on clothes—they like to give their fans an inside look!

As much as Leo loves their loud prints and wild outfits, you're actually much more likely to run into them wearing something very polished. They love tailored pieces, as well as their signature metal, gold. Leo is the lion . . . like any cat, they know intuitively whether they want their head scratched by you or whether they would rather turn away and look out the window to something else more interesting . . . so *be* interesting. Don't be afraid to be yourself or stand out from the crowd. Leo loathes a poseur, but falls head over heels for someone who isn't afraid to do their own thing.

FLIRTING TECHNIQUES

Yes, Leo loves compliments; however, being pursued too hard is a huge turn-off for them. They enjoy winning someone over, so when you first meet them, playing it cool and aloof will leave a bigger impression than fawning all over them, or worse, showing off your muscles—let *them* show off to *you*.

Leo is truly a big cat. When you first meet a cat you would like to befriend, do you shove a toy in its face, chase it around the house, and demand to pick it up? No! You give it space. The fastest way to make a cat your friend is to be aloof, and then they'll be on your lap in no time. It's the same with Leo. Of course, this doesn't mean they don't love to be courted, complimented, and catered to. You just need to be cool. Leo loves flirting, so keep the banter light and keep the spotlight shining on them, not you; don't chat with them about your vacation plans—ask them about *theirs*.

Leo is a sign that loves to have a good time, so show them how fun, generous, and creative you are—buy a round of drinks for your friends at the bar, host a fantastic party, invite them to a gallery show you're a part of, and casually introduce them to well-known people in your scene. Leo loves meeting new people and enjoys feeling connected. If you can boost their social life in some way, that will pique their interest.

Leos either love or hate PDA—you'll have to find out which sort of Leo they are. Leos who love PDA will gladly show off their romance to everyone, but the kind who avoid PDA usually, like celebrities do, dislike them because they want their space and privacy—people gossip about them so much, you know. Give them plenty of verbal affirmation while still giving them some space, allowing them to miss you and chase after you.

DATING STYLE

If you have the means to whisk your Leo lover away to an exotic location, do it—Leo loves spending time in paradise, documenting their journeys in photos to show their friends at home, not to mention having sex on the beach during a spectacular sunset. So dramatic! If travel isn't something you can pull off for Leo just yet, take them someplace fabulous, where people go to be seen and mingle with the rich and famous. Leo loves to party, so take them to one.

A group date where you know the participants will be open to talking about sex, religion, and politics is also a good idea. Leo loves to connect with intellectuals and share ideas with new friends. Leo thinks they want dramatic, long-stemmed roses and candlelit dinners, but in truth, they just want to party, have fun, share stories, and live life—those long-stemmed roses will get destroyed after Leo's night bar-hopping. But that doesn't mean your Leo lover doesn't want a nice bouquet every now and then! Be sure to treat your Leo to some romantic gestures.

RELATIONSHIP APPROACH

Leo loves security—they are a fixed sign, after all, so they're wonderful partners. They stay true to their word and, as much as they love to party, Leos are generally responsible people. Loyal and honorable, Leos are incredibly trustworthy partners who will treat you with respect. They're looking for someone who will rule right next to them, and they know how to treat their queen or king. As possessive and jealous as Leo can be sometimes, they can easily feel compassion for their lovers, making them a great fit for a polyamorous relationship. Leo just wants everyone to be happy!

However, there is a side to Leo that can be frustrating. For many Leos, the best part of romance is falling in love . . . then, it's all downhill if the flirtation, the chase, the drama, or the excitement ends. Flirting is one of the things that keeps Leo alive, so you must keep the mystery going. Invite them out for a date, but keep the location a surprise (that said, take them someplace you know they adore—Leo can be quite picky!). Mental stimulation is important to them. They like to argue and debate, as long as no one is getting seriously hurt. Leo loves to shout because it helps them get out their fiery passion, but the last thing the cuddly lion wants to do is make someone cry.

As outgoing as they are, they also really need to spend time alone. It's crucial that Leo has space to reflect on their needs, as well as to have time to be creative. Leo has a lot to give—but if they're always performing onstage, when will they have time to mess around in the studio?

It is rare to get a second chance with Leo, especially if you hurt their pride. Once they've dumped you, you won't be welcomed back into the fold. That said, if you dump them, and they feel that you were just too inexperienced, unintelligent, or unintuitive to see what you had, they'll gladly take you back once you've come to your senses and realized that they're the only one for you . . . if only to save face. Leo hates to be humiliated! So, if you want a Leo back, be prepared to eat some humble pie.

SEX

There are two sides to Leo. One side loves drama; therefore, they love sex—the mystery, the anticipation, the intensity of a first kiss, the thrill of a make-up fuck. Sex is another opportunity to live life—and Leo loves to *live*. Create a passionate and romantic environment with flowers, silk sheets, plenty of candlelight, and music to set the mood. If the setting looks like it could potentially be on the cover of a romance novel, you're good.

But if you've ever observed the state of pure bliss a meditating cat radiates, then you know there is a mystical side to Leo—they are royalty, and in many cultures throughout history, that meant they were connected to the gods!—one that's eager for connection to realms beyond the material. Behind Leo's love of materialism, sex—whether it's during masturbation or with someone they deeply care about—creates a portal for them to connect with a higher power, to their partner's spirit, or to their own inner voice.

TURN-ONS

The ultimate pillow queen, Leo wants to lay back and relax while you worship their body. In fact, the more, the merrier! Bring some friends to help you fan and feed them like royalty while they lounge on their throne. Speaking of pillows, make sure they are silk or velvet (preferably a passionate red or royal blue). Leo wants to be in luxury!

The submissive Leo may enjoy scenes and roles where they can lay back and be stroked. Experiment with BDSM because the gentle lion may enjoy performing acts for their partner—or spankings, if done correctly! However, when Leo is the dominant one, they can easily take the role of king or queen with their servant, leading to some hot power-play actions.

Whether your Leo lover is dominant or submissive, they need to feel like they are the center of attention. This is especially true in a group sex scenario. Take sexy Polaroids of them or bring a mirror into the bedroom. They're exhibitionists, and while not every Leo is an outdoors person (some absolutely love it, while others wouldn't be caught dead camping in the woods), a make-out session in a park will usually get them going. Bending them over in a bar bathroom is a spontaneous and striking move any Leo can appreciate.

Be dramatic. Moan, grunt, put on a show—but more importantly, make it clear that you're enjoying the *Leo Show*: tell them you love seeing, hearing, feeling them get off. Leo also loves the satisfaction of getting you off, so communicate. Tell them what you want, so they can prove their prowess to you.

Remember, Leo rules the heart, so tell them yours will break if you can't have them right then and there. Leo loves make-up sex, and the drama of coming together after a difficult time is totally thrilling to them.

TURN-OFFS

Nothing will kill a Leo's mood more than being criticized! Their favorite part of lovemaking is feeling beautiful and cared for, and don't ever forget it.

Playing it cool works for getting their attention, but not in bed.

Sex that feels like a chore is their signal that the passion has died. Expect them to either whip up some drama or to dump you.

LEO & ARIES

Leo might be royalty, but Aries is a conqueror. If these two signs are on the same team, they're an unbeatable pair, but if they are on differing sides, it can be the showdown of the century!

These two Fire signs have plenty of fun together. They're both excited about exploring the world and have a similar desire for inspiration in their lives. Leo is very impressed by Aries's intellect and the stories they tell about the adventures they have been on. Aries has plenty of fun with Leo and loves attending the many parties the lion gets invited to. They both enjoy arguing—it helps Aries release tension, and Leo loves a bit of drama; however, a healthy debate can cross into unhealthy territory if these two are not careful.

"Aloof" isn't usually a word to describe Aries in love; however, they would be wise to be cool around Leo, because coming on too strong is a turn-off for the lion. Leo would be wise to share the spotlight—to share everything, really—because Aries desires a partner who can compromise and who isn't greedy. Aries is okay with spoiled and vain, but greedy is a major turn-off.

Their energy in bed is hot, especially the first time, when they have such a strong desire to impress each other. After that, it's important that their kinks align and that they keep communication open. If they move in together, Leo will see a softer, more sensitive side to Aries, and Aries will also see a more emotional, even spiritual, side to Leo.

LEO & TAURUS

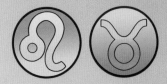

Leo and Taurus are both loyal, dependable, and creative people. What could go wrong? Well, they're also both stubborn, so it's possible that at the first sign of a disagreement, these two may decide not to move things forward. Leo does not want a lover who is lazy, which Taurus can sometimes be in bed, and Taurus doesn't want a partner who needs the attention on themself all the time. However, if these two have enough sexual chemistry, they'll be willing to put their differences aside to see what a night between the sheets will be like. And between Leo's fire and Taurus's slow, seductive sensuality, their night together will be as hot as the Sun and Venus.

If their chemistry works and they're able to compromise, this can be a partnership that challenges them both to be their best selves. They will be rewarded with a lover who values security and loyalty as much as they do. Taurus feels very at home with luxurious, opulent Leo, and Leo admires Taurus's creativity, looking to them for inspiration in their creative work.

Leo would be wise to reveal their vulnerabilities to Taurus—acting like they are cooler than everyone, all the time, will not impress Taurus, a sign that needs to be with someone who has more dimensions than "famous." Taurus needs to show Leo that they can think outside the box, that they can be a rebel from time to time. If they live together, they'll continue to motivate each other, as long as they make efforts to compromise. Enjoying life's pleasures comes easily to them, so after any difficult compromise, they should reward themself with a luxurious dinner.

LEO & GEMINI

Leo loves a compliment, and Gemini is fantastic at providing verbal affirmations, so these two will easily be off to a good start. Leo is also endlessly entertaining, which is a plus for Gemini, a sign that doesn't like to get bored and who is in love with a creative mind. These two have a strong intellectual connection—Leo thinks Gemini is a visionary and loves meeting their friends and going to parties with them. Gemini is turned on by Leo's creative and intellectual brilliance and loves the community Leo cultivates around them.

But it's not all sunshine and party invites. If Leo is in a phase of life where they believe no one is good enough and that someone better is just around the corner, or if Gemini is in a fickle phase, things won't go anywhere, not even to the bedroom. When this happens, neither will "stoop"

to being the one to take initiative when they believe it's the other that should do the courting.

If they do make it to the bedroom, the energy will be hot—Leo's passion and drama will excite Gemini, who is willing to try anything Leo might come up with. Their elements are Fire and Air—two elements that feed each other. Expect sparks. Leo would be wise to stay open-minded and to avoid bratty behavior, and Gemini should show their smarts and inventiveness if they want to continue to win Leo over. If they move in together, Leo needs to be mindful not to annex Gemini's office space, and Gemini needs to respect whatever superstitions Leo holds. Neither should judge the other for gossiping—they just like to be in the know!

LEO & CANCER

The Sun and Moon—a most iconic pair, don't you think? They have their differences, but we would be lost without them. However, would Leo and Cancer be lost without each other? They'd be surprised to find how close they can become once they get over any initial differences. Family is very important to them both, and so are loyalty, security, creativity, and self-expression. Leo might seem more outgoing, and Cancer more shy, but the truth is they both have their moods. Cancer enjoys time onstage sharing their talents, and Leo longs to hide in the studio, working on their art. But as long as they respect one another and give each other space, these two can become each other's worlds.

In the bedroom, Cancer's sensitivity and imagination blend with Leo's heart and flair for drama. This is an intense coupling for a one-night stand. Leo finds Cancer to be totally mysterious, which draws them in but can also leave them confused. Cancer admires Leo's confidence, but may also be hurt by Leo's self-absorption. If they want things to work, Leo needs to be their most mature self for Cancer, and when Cancer needs space for a few hours (or days), they have to help Leo understand that they aren't ditching them. If they decide to move in together, Cancer will be pleased to get to know a more emotional side to Leo, as well as be let in on a secret or two, and Leo will also get a chance to know the enigmatic Cancer on a deeper level.

LEO & LEO

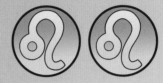

Two Leos means two giant hearts and two massive egos. They're loyal to each other, fun loving (they always have a reason to celebrate), and share many of the same dreams and values. They're each one of the coolest people either of them has ever met, but like two cats who are introduced for the first time, they might have to get used to each other initially. Sniff each other out. Share a meal. They take their time, circling each other, learning more about each other's goals and standards. And if they fall in love, they'll have met the royal match they have been looking for.

A friends-with-benefits situation can work, so long as neither of them is working through a very jealous phase in their life. The energy in the bedroom is passionate, so expect plenty of fireworks and excitement—they like an over-the-top vibe between the sheets. They're both very theatrical, and they really don't care if the neighbors can hear them. From heavily making out under an umbrella while waiting for a cab to playfully touching each other at a restaurant, everyone can see this couple's explosive chemistry.

They both pride themselves on being fair and logical people who are open to healthy debates (or dramatically splashing a drink in someone's face, whatever seems right), and they both need a home to retreat to that feels safe and secure. They enjoy spontaneous nights on the town, and a surprise dinner date is never a bad idea.

LEO & VIRGO

Leo doesn't shy away from sharing their thoughts or displaying their talents, but Virgo still finds them to be one of the most enigmatic people they have ever met. Virgo sees a very deep side of Leo—a side many people miss. Leo, though straightforward, has a lot they don't show the world, too, so Virgo's respect and understanding of their private side is something Leo appreciates. Leo admires many things about Virgo—their work ethic, practicality, and connection to nature. Virgo cares about helping people, which is something Leo really respects. If a superstar doesn't give back, what's the point in having all that fame and success?

Virgo would be wise to show their intellect and commitment to social causes. Leo would be smart to display their creative side, as well as their flexibility and adaptability, like mutable Virgo. The energy in the bedroom is intense—Leo's flair for drama excites lusty Virgo, who is eager to explore anything Leo is curious about.

These two signs are very different people, but they appreciate each other's perspectives. They know that the other can see things that they can't see too clearly themself, so they really appreciate one another's opinions. If they decide to move in together, they would be wise to continue exploring spirituality together, perhaps building a meditation room to share after Leo's long days being the center of attention and Virgo's ambitious days helping the world.

LEO & LIBRA

Leo and Libra are two signs accused of spending too much time in the mirror (they can't help it, they're beautiful), but they have so much more depth than that—Libra is genuinely concerned with justice, and Leo genuinely desires to be a strong leader.

They have so much to offer the world, and they see greatness in each other. Leo admires Libra's mind and doesn't get annoyed when Libra is indecisive. Instead, Leo grabs some popcorn and watches Libra deliberate, learning from Libra's fantastic and intellectual mind. Libra is inspired by Leo's vision for the future, as well as how they treat their friends and tend to their social circles and communities. And romance—they both crave romance. They love drama, romantic red roses, perfumed love letters, late-night phone calls, and early-morning kisses after evenings of intense passion. Libra's seductive energy blends beautifully with Leo's drama in the bedroom. A big mirror should be kept by the bed. If they move in together, they should probably hang one from the ceiling, too.

These two become best friends easily, and a casual sexual relationship can work well between them, thanks to their fantastic communication skills. Leo would be wise to take charge from time to time, relieving Libra from the decision fatigue that sometimes sets in. Libra would be wise to show how loyal they are—it's something Leo deeply craves in a partner!

LEO & SCORPIO

Sunny Leo and brooding Scorpio have loads of tension between them, but they have so much to learn from each other. The first thing Leo will learn from Scorpio is that the scorpion isn't going to take any bullshit on Leo's part. If Leo says they'll swing by after work but calls a few minutes after they are supposed to meet to let Scorpio know there's a party instead, that isn't going to fly. If Leo thinks dependability is important to them, they'll soon realize it's even more important to Scorpio.

The first thing Scorpio will learn about the royal lion is that when Leo says they need space, they mean it—and Scorpio shouldn't snoop around. Privacy is important to Scorpio, and it's just as important to Leo. They have different communication styles, but once they get over that hump, these two will deliver all the passion they both need. It's crucial they continue to affirm their love for each other, both verbally and nonverbally. Everything from *I love you* messages to acts of service will prove their devotion to one another.

The energy in the bedroom is very intense—Leo's fire and Scorpio's sex appeal make for a steamy combination. Scorpio would be wise to show Leo that they're not afraid to stand out from the crowd and that they're committed to self-improvement—not just in the sense of making more money or staying fit, but emotionally and spiritually as well. Leo would be wise to show Scorpio that they're creative. Even though Leo is a creative spirit, this royal sign doesn't always share the behind-the-scenes creative process with people, but if Scorpio sees this, they'll feel much closer to Leo. Leo should display their calm side, too. As much as Leo loves a spectacle, they also have a side that is quiet and collected and rarely seen, and this is a side Scorpio benefits from getting to know and love. If they move in together, Leo will easily feel at home with Scorpio, and Scorpio will look up to Leo for innovative inspiration.

125

LEO & SAGITTARIUS

The heat between two Fire signs is a bright and burning one, but how long can the flame live? Well, even a short fling will bring memorable sparks, and these two make great casual sexual partners or a fun one-night stand.

Things flow so smoothly between them that it's possibly *too* easy—Leo needs drama and passion, and they don't really want to flirt with someone who doesn't give them plenty of butterflies. Sagittarius would be wise to be aloof around Leo—this big cat is curious about people who are a little out of reach. As for turning Sagittarius on, Leo should show how socially connected and intellectual they are. These two not only have a fantastic time partying and traveling together, but they also share a deep desire for spiritual connection—Sagittarius is always seeking wisdom and Leo benefits deeply from a daily meditation practice.

Leo is a very romantic sign, but what Sagittarius makes them realize is that they actually love an adventure or an intellectually stimulating conversation even more than they care about a box of Godivas or diamond rings. If these two move in together, they'll certainly get to see a more sensitive, emotional side to one another. Gratitude is a theme that's major in this relationship: they'll thrive if they practice it, but if they're snobby, stuck-up, or spoiled, they won't.

LEO & CAPRICORN

Leo is ruled by the Sun, and Capricorn by Saturn: These two heavenly bodies are far from each other, but when the two signs get close, things get interesting. Leo's warmth and Capricorn's cool, earthy vibe blend together for a union that's intense. Leo pushes Capricorn to face their fears and opens them up for an even deeper intimacy than they could have imagined. Capricorn challenges Leo to get their crap together—no more chain smoking while finishing up a project three hours before it is time to be handed in. They have so much to learn from each other, and while this relationship will require them both to make adjustments, when the sign of royalty and the boss of the zodiac come together, they can make amazing things happen.

Between the sheets, Leo's love of drama is met by Capricorn's often kinky, always lusty approach to lovemaking. Their communication styles differ, so it's important that they communicate openly about what they want—Leo should not be afraid to talk about their wildest dreams, and Capricorn shouldn't be shy about asking hard questions. (Capricorn isn't afraid of much, but they do try to be delicate about sensitive issues . . . especially with someone who can be as theatrical as Leo!) Leo's warmth is very attractive to Capricorn, no matter how emotionally distant Capricorn may seem at first, so Leo would be wise not to hide this side of themself in an effort to win Capricorn over—it won't work. Capricorn dislikes anyone who is fake, anyway. Capricorn should be authentic, too—Leo wants a partner who is not afraid to be true to themself. If they live together, they'll need plenty of space to display their awards, medals, certificates, and diplomas.

LEO & AQUARIUS

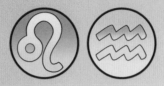

They are the two coolest signs in the zodiac: Leo is more of a cachet cool, warm and popular, and Aquarius is a contrarian kind, cool and rebellious. They're opposites (literally, they oppose each other on the zodiac wheel), but they do have at least one thing in common—they're extreme people, with Leo being very fiery and Aquarius being so logical. They'll either get along famously (because *famous* is how Leo does everything, of course) or be totally bored by each other. They're both strong-willed, which means they can be stubborn, but they're very reliable partners. As long as Leo communicates honestly, especially when they're upset (instead of letting it brew, which they may do because they can be intimidated by Aquarius's sometimes chilly demeanor), and Aquarius makes an effort to be polite and diplomatic, things can work out. They both need verbal affirmation and plenty of communication, but they also need to see action to go with words, especially words like *I love you.*

Cool Aquarius is entertained by Leo's theatrics, and Leo thinks Aquarius is the perfect person to bounce creative ideas off of. Their sense of humor is different, but they both like meeting people who can show them new ways of laughing, as well as new ideas. At home, Leo craves privacy and a space to feel their emotions—Aquarius totally respects this. Leo will be quite surprised by Aquarius's decorating skills! Aquarius is certainly stylish—they're not afraid to have their own unique look, and Leo will enjoy the eccentric taste Aquarius brings to the home. And what about the bedroom? Between the sheets, plenty of dirty talk keeps things hot. Leo brings drama, and Aquarius loves having a sexy show to watch.

LEO & PISCES

If Leo is looking for drama and excitement, they don't need to look any further than Pisces, whose imagination can spin endless adventures for them to go on. These two signs have a lot to learn from each other—sensitive and empathetic Pisces encourages Leo to open up to transformation, to let go of their past pain, and to face their fears. Leo inspires Pisces to get their act together—to build supportive routines and to practice self-care. *Boundaries* are an important theme for this couple, and they need to learn how to give and take freely and fairly, without exhausting each other. Pisces is always willing to lend an ear, and Leo is a very generous sign.

Between the sheets, the energy is intense, as Pisces's psychic energy mingles with Leo's fiery drama in a potent way. Pisces would be wise to show their wild and weird side to Leo (not just in bed, but out! Leo loves someone who stands out from the crowd). Leo should be flexible with Pisces (again, not just in bed—although Pisces wouldn't mind seeing Leo in a few revealing positions—but also in life), as Leo can be quite stubborn. If these two signs decide to keep this relationship a short-term fling, it will be intense. They're likely to learn a lot from each other, even if they only spend a short time together. Long term, if they decide to move in together, they'll enjoy working on creative projects as a couple and are sure to throw fantastic parties. Leo might be more dramatic than Pisces, but that doesn't mean Pisces doesn't know how to let loose.

VIRGO

THE MAIDEN

DATES: AUGUST 23–SEPTEMBER 23

PLANETARY RULER: MERCURY
ELEMENT: EARTH
MODALITY: MUTABLE

PERSONALITY

Deep in the woods, squirrels are burying acorns, bees are buzzing, a fox is on the hunt, and a tree houses a flock of sparrows. To some, this may seem like chaos, but to Virgo, all of this is in perfect balance: each animal and plant plays its part.

An Earth sign, Virgo, in a word, is practical. Ruled by Mercury, Virgo is all about communication and assessment of information. As a mutable sign, Virgo is the last sign in their season—in this case, summer. They are the analysts of the zodiac, taking critical notice of small details, hardworking, and eager to be of service.

Purity is a key feature of Virgo, but Virgo isn't just the perfectionist that pop astrology would have you believe. Yes, they know that practice makes perfect, but they're also on another search: the search for self-discovery. Learning who they are and how they can be of service to the world is a major part of their destiny. How does love fit into all of this?

AT THEIR BEST

Analytical, productive, prudent Virgo has a fantastic work ethic, and is witty with a keen eye for details. Diligent Virgo is an excellent helper and loves being of service to others. Young at heart, Virgo is modest, gentle, and thoughtful. Virgo loves animals and nature, and though this sign is often associated with perfection, Virgo knows in their heart that flawlessness can be found in the design of the universe; therefore, we are all perfect.

AT THEIR WORST

Virgo never outgrew their awkward phase, and these self-pitying control freaks are overly critical nitpickers who often hold others to a higher standard than they hold themself. Calculating, they overthink everything, and can have trouble minding their own business. Secretive, skeptical, and petty, Virgo can also be a cynic and a hypochondriac. They can be as messy as they are fussy.

LOVE PERSONALITY

Purity is certainly a theme tied to the energy of Virgo; however, don't be fooled by their name. Virgo is an Earth sign, and they are very physical—and very lusty. They love to connect with others, intellectually *and* sexually, and these cerebral people can even flow with no strings attached when the mood strikes. But Virgo does fall in love . . . and when they do, it's deep and long-lasting.

Virgo takes love seriously: They approach romance like they do their work, which is to say, with total focus and responsibility. They throw themself fully into it! And they expect the same in return—someone who will be there for them emotionally and physically. As reliable a partner as Virgo is when they are in love, one thing to realize about this deep-thinking sign is that they do need their time alone— it helps them recharge and stay creative. When the right balance between space and togetherness is struck, Virgo is able to thrive.

Not much is a mystery to down-to-earth, logical, grounded Virgo . . . but love is, and they like it that way. There's a mystical side to Virgo that is often overlooked by astrologers; there is a part of them that can speak to nature and connect with the cosmos—they're not sure how it all makes sense, but it *works*. Love is part of this same spiritual side to Virgo's life. And as much as they appreciate their solitude, they also crave deep connection.

FIRST IMPRESSIONS

Virgos often keep to themselves, yet end up in the busiest places. If you meet them in a pub, you'll probably see them sitting off to a corner with a cocktail, reading a book, rather than schmoozing at the bar. Online, you'll notice how particular they are about when, how, and where you meet. Virgos aren't always the easiest people to approach—they're busy, you know! But when you do make eye contact, you'll see that this person who often keeps to themself has a bit of a trickster's sparkle in their eye; they are youthful, and, once the ice is broken, as friendly as they are helpful.

They're clearly smart. When you look at them, you can tell there is a lot of inner dialogue going on. Virgo is an intellectual, and loves to talk about the *real* meaning behind whatever art, current event, or idea they're inspired by at the moment. Their clothing style has a chic, utilitarian vibe to it, and they like to keep things simple (though they do like to mess around with their hair, beards, and makeup).

FLIRTING TECHNIQUES

Intellectual connection is very important to Virgo. Virgo loves to flirt, but they like to flirt with someone who is sharp and witty. As serious and dedicated to their work as they may be, they are also seduced by people who are *cool*—those in a scene, VIPs at local venues, or those in the know.

Self-conscious Virgo is always a little surprised when someone unexpectedly hits on them. *Me?* they ask. They may not respond to you out of fear that you meant to call out to the person behind them or that you texted the wrong number. Call them by their name when you flirt, so they know you're talking to them. Make them feel *seen*.

Virgo works hard, and like anyone who spends a lot of time being presentable, responsible, and professional, Virgo likes to really have *fun*. They live by the motto "play hard, work hard." When texting with your Virgo, send lots of dirty messages (inject some humor, as they love a good dirty joke!) and nudes, but be sure to have good lighting, please! And no dirty socks on the floor!

DATING STYLE

Much has been said about hardworking Virgo being the sign of service and purity. But, trust me, they do like to let their hair down. Whisk them away for a weekend exploring a beautiful beach, traipsing about in a city, or dancing the night away. Virgo also appreciates historic places, filled with stories, so spend a day with them at the museum, or have a drink together at the oldest tavern nearby. Virgo likes to stay up-to-date about art and culture—less so with pop culture, but definitely the avant-garde, underground, and up-and-coming—so visit a gallery together or go see a concert by an artist they admire.

Virgo loves a routine; however, that doesn't mean they don't want to try something new. A date where they get to learn a new skill, as well as smooch with you, is their idea of fun. Perhaps a day at an archery range or indoor rock climbing? Pottery making is also a Virgo aphrodisiac.

Virgos are born event planners: plan a group dinner for close friends where you two decide on the location, caterers, music, decor, invitations—the whole to-do!

RELATIONSHIP APPROACH

Whether you're in a polyamorous or a monogamous relationship with Virgo, scheduling is extremely important. You'll find a shared online calendar to be very helpful. Scheduling time for one another is very important to Virgo, not just because they are control freaks who need to know what they're doing and when, but also because they like the emotional security of being in a routine with the people they love.

Many people think the concept of a routine and romance are incompatible; however, it's through consistent practice, routine, and ritual that magic happens. When we can schedule time to connect with the people we love, we're able to stay grounded in such a busy world that's filled with texts, tweets, and status updates. Routine doesn't need to be something that's forced onto a relationship—Virgo likes seeing how a routine will naturally fall into place with someone, which is something that can take time, but is worth it to them. They're spontaneous, too. Because they have such packed schedules, if they can randomly see you for a coffee between gigs, they'll love it.

Virgos do like to check in throughout the day, so sending a message to ask them how their day is going is very much appreciated. Virgo is the sign of service, so you can bet that they'll be there for you. Return the favor by being there for them, especially to help them unwind and relax, perhaps by rubbing their feet at the end of the day or cooking them a delicious and healthy meal. Just don't try to clean up their office for them as a surprise while they're away—their desk might be disorganized, but they know where everything is!

Flexibility within relationships is really important to Virgo—just as important as routine. They know that even the strongest bridge will collapse if it's too rigid, so some sway is needed. If flexibility isn't given, the less mature Virgo may fib or cheat to maintain the front that everything is under control, while the more mature Virgo has the confidence and communication skills to discuss their needs when they come up.

SEX

Virgo loves a wholesome vibe, but that doesn't mean that they're not going to feel you up while you two are watching TV under the quilt their grandmother sewed.

So much of Virgo's life is measured and controlled; they're very analytical people. However, sex and masturbation are opportunities for them to step away from their controlled lives. Sex is a time to be in the moment, to express their heart's desires without overanalyzing them, and to really be alive. Spontaneity turns them on.

Virgo is the sign of service, and that certainly extends to the bedroom, where they're very eager to please their lovers and to explore their own sexual needs.

To help Virgo get in the mood, pitch in to get their chores and tasks done so they don't have something nagging at them when they want to unwind. Walking in on you cleaning the counter might be enough to get them going—Virgo has been known to feel up their sweetheart while they do the dishes.

TURN-ONS

Virgos are very tactile individuals. Massage is a wonderful way to get Virgo to unwind and be in the mood. They do so much for others, so ask what you can do for them. Virgo does like variety, so keep things interesting by trying new positions and finding different ways to pleasure each other.

They are particular people, so don't be surprised if they have a very specific kink! Your submissive Virgo wants to worship and be a slave to you, while the more dominant Virgo will likely want to brand or take ownership of you in some way—sub or dom, they take on the roles of boss or servant quite well. Virgo wants to do a good job! Be sure to reward them when they do. Virgo loves uniforms, so don't toss out your sexy nurse or sailor outfit from Halloween. (Well, unless it has stains all over it from fake zombie ooze; in that case, toss it out! Virgo hates a mess.)

As visual people, they can be voyeurs; however, some- times they aren't watching because it turns them on, but simply because they're curious how other people do it! Virgo can be a little nosy!

Virgo often likes the glossy, porn star look, as well as man- icured hands and groomed body hair. Sex parties excite Virgo; even if they don't participate, they'll usually have fun watching, and will enjoy doing something naughty, if only for the novelty. Adventure is more important to Virgo than many realize—any activity that's focused on trying something new with someone they love is a turn-on.

TURN-OFFS

Sexual health is very important to Virgo. Being irresponsible about this is a huge turn-off.

Despite being a mutable sign, in many ways, Virgo can be very rigid and a perfectionist. However, in bed, it's very important for things to be flexible. If you only have one way that you like to do things, this may not work for them in the long term.

Virgo loves a quickie, but *sloppy* they don't do: be showered, sober, and honest about your wants and needs, physically and emotionally.

Running into an old lover while they are working is their biggest nightmare. If you pick your Virgo lover up after work and they're rattled after having seen their ex at a meeting, give them some time to decompress.

VIRGO & ARIES

Analytical Virgo knows a lot about data ... but what about belief? Do they believe in true love? How about true love at first sight? These are the sorts of questions Aries will dare them to answer during a game of truth or dare. Virgo will complain that they picked *dare*, not *truth*, but Aries will disagree, knowing that they can do whatever they want with a dare—it'll be the first of a few disagreements between these two! These two signs challenge each other, but Virgo is turned on by Aries's passionate fire—it stirs something deep ... something sexy and *real* ... within them. And Aries is also excited about Virgo, a sign that's a blend of logical and artistic.

Aries would be wise to be a little more laid-back around Virgo, who could get turned off by the ram's impatience and bad temper. Virgo can be very critical—*not* something Aries cares for in a relationship—and needs to be more diplomatic around the ram.

There is a lot of intensity between these two signs: Aries pushes Virgo to confront difficult questions they didn't even realize they needed to ask themself, and Virgo pushes Aries to ditch their bad habits. As a result, they can make a lot of amazing transformations with each other. Out in the world, Aries encourages and appreciates Virgo's more wacky hobbies and interests, and in bed, they both have a thirst for new adventures—their lovemaking styles are certainly different, and getting to know each other should be exciting for both parties.

VIRGO & TAURUS

When soft, sensual Taurus meets cool, analytical Virgo, they're pleased to meet someone who is so similar, yet so different. Flexible Virgo can make anything happen, and so can Taurus—not through analytical skill or adaptability, but with determination. Virgo and Taurus often end up in the same place but have a totally different way of getting there—can they take the journey through life together?

It depends: Although Taurus has so much fun with Virgo and is creatively inspired by them, and Virgo is motivated by Taurus's philosophies and their cultured, well-traveled lifestyle, Taurus needs to prove to Virgo that they can be flexible as well—or at least sometimes. And Virgo needs to prove to Taurus that they can keep a promise.

Virgo's imagination in bed blends beautifully with the sensual passion Taurus exudes. If they decide to live together, the following is some wisdom to help keep things cool in the long run: Communication-planet Mercury rules Virgo, so Virgo should be sure to talk about Taurus's favorite thing, which, being ruled by Venus, is beauty. But don't just talk about how beautiful Taurus is—although of course Taurus loves to hear it—but also about the good that they see in the world. Virgo likes to complain, which is fine with Taurus—up to a point. The complaining needs to be punctuated with some positivity—not phony, wishful thinking positivity, but real reflections on meaningful, beautiful things. If Virgo is stuck and can't think of something nice to say, perhaps Taurus should take their hand and go for a walk in the woods. These two both love nature and see its beauty.

VIRGO & GEMINI

They're both ruled by Mercury, so they get each other on a deep, deep level: the curiosity, the need for detail, the nervousness, the excitement. Virgo is a touch more grounded than Gemini, and Gemini is a little more outgoing than Virgo, but chances are, they appreciate these differences in one another and do not feel intimidated or bothered by them.

There is a lot of tension between these two, which makes for plenty of sparks in bed, where they'll both find their match in terms of versatility and eagerness to please. When one of these two says, "I want to explore your body," it's more than just a cheesy pickup line; they will literally and thoroughly please each part of the other's body—neither of these signs wants to hear "You missed a spot" after any kind of activity.

Virgo's whole vibe is one that Gemini feels very comfortable with—their work ethic, their love of nature, their independent streak, as well as their desire to help people. Virgo looks up to Gemini, admires them for their sociability and their fantastic ideas—Virgo is very attracted to cool people, and Gemini is certainly a popular, social butterfly. These two can make amazing things happen by how much they inspire and support each other, but if they want to make things even better between them, Virgo should show their free-spirited and adventurous side. Virgo might seem rigid at times, but they have it in them to go a bit wild! Gemini should display their intuitive and empathetic abilities (they're very logical people, and this might not come naturally to them; however, they have it in them, too!). These signs know that anything is possible when you have the right ingredients, the right tools. So this love can totally succeed as long as they communicate and care.

VIRGO & CANCER

Virgo has always been fascinated by the Moon, Cancer's ruling planet. The phases, its pull on the tides, its rumored effect on werewolves and increased hospital visits. The Moon is exciting! And so, Cancer excites Virgo, too. Cancer is someone Virgo wants to be around. They admire their taste and their social connections, and they also appreciate their commitment to their community. Virgo believes being of service to the world is important, and no one is more nurturing than the crab.

Cancer admires Virgo's analytical mind, their cool, rational, down-to-earth vibe. Cancer would be wise to show their sense of adventure and curiosity, how they long to see the world beyond their shell. In return, Virgo should display how mature and accomplished they are, because it makes Cancer feel safe.

Their energy in the bedroom is dynamic. Virgo's versatility meets Cancer's intuition. They're both eager to try new things, and because their communication styles are compatible, Virgo and Cancer can talk about the kinkiest things without feeling awkward. They're good friends, so something casual could work, but they'll need to be clear about where they stand in the relationship, including whether or not they're seeing other people. Virgo might expect to hear all the details about Cancer's other conquests, while Cancer might think it's none of their business, which could lead to some hurt feelings if they don't keep the lines of communication open about their boundaries. If they decide to move in together, Cancer will create a nurturing environment that Virgo will be diligent about keeping neat and tidy.

VIRGO & LEO

Virgo and Leo are very different, but that doesn't stop them from being best friends—they learn so much from each other and share a fantastic sense of humor. Of course, when they fight—it's bad. Virgo knows how to put someone in their place and Leo knows drama. If Virgo is too pessimistic or critical or if Leo is snobby, this union won't go anywhere. But as long as they get along, they'll have a great time. Virgo can make sure they stay on good terms by complimenting Leo . . . a lot . . . like, more than Virgo probably already does or thinks is necessary! And Leo should show they're appreciative of all the hard work Virgo does for them.

Virgo is on a search for self-discovery, and being around Leo teaches them a lot about themself—they appreciate the insight. Leo has a lot of pride, but they still feel shaky in their confidence from time to time—they are only human, after all—and Virgo knows how to lift them out of any funks and teach them a lot about self-worth.

Virgo's versatility in the bedroom is thrilling for theatrical Leo. Leo's fire and Virgo's earthly sensuality blend remarkably well. They often give each other pleasure and ideas that they didn't even think of exploring. This can be an intense coupling as a one-night stand, but they can do a casual long-term relationship quite easily, as long as neither of them is in a jealous phase of life. Long term, if they decide to move in together, they'll both learn more about each other's spiritual sides. Leo would be wise to show Virgo how flexible they can be, as well as show their loyal heart. Virgo should show Leo that even though they like to follow the instruction manual that came with their latest gadget, they're also not afraid to think outside the box.

VIRGO & VIRGO

There are three kinds of Virgos: The sort who say, "I'm so stressed out. I'm not in the mood to make love." The kind who say, "I'm so stressed out, I need to make love." And the ones who say, "What do making love or being stressed out have to do with each other?" The success of this relationship, whether it's a commitment or a casual friends-with-benefits situation, depends on whether or not they share the same attitude.

These two both have a straightforward communication style—intuitive, yet practical—and they know how to read between the lines. Verbal affirmations and open communication are very important to them, but so is their space and having time to recharge. They're both very particular people, so if they fall in love, you can bet that these two will set and meet high standards for each other.

When they party, they like to really let loose, and they have a devilish side to them as well—one that the public doesn't see. In a partner, they both crave someone who is empathetic and artistic, a deep thinker *and* a deep feeler. In bed, they appreciate spontaneity, sparks, excitement—they feel *alive* between the sheets!

In their social lives, they're very caring about the people they get close to and are very protective of their friends, so they should make an effort to get along with each other's crew. If they decide to move in together, they are going to be one of those couples that has a map with pins stuck to mark all the places they want to visit together—if not a map of the whole world, then at least a map of all the pizza places, art supply stores, secret gardens, or whatever hobby they're currently passionate about!

VIRGO & LIBRA

There is a thin line between love and hate, and these two know this well. When Virgo first met Libra, they didn't know if they wanted to *be* them, be *with* them, or couldn't stand them—a lot of feelings were involved, like envy and admiration.

Libra has a lot to teach Virgo about self-worth, but Virgo has plenty to teach Libra, too. Like not ignoring facts when they're right in front of their face, and confronting difficult parts of themself. Virgo sees Libra's blind spots and, as Virgo does, will plainly let them know what they have been missing. This will either freak Libra out or they will be grateful that Virgo let them know that they had, metaphorically, spinach in their teeth. Communication skills are important—especially *listening* skills, and these two need to be able to listen to each other if they want things to work out.

Libra would be wise to display their artistic talents to Virgo, and Virgo should show Libra how they can take charge. Neither of them should be fake or passive-aggressive with the other—it will start major drama! These two often share a fantastic sense of humor—if they have that, this can be a great pair. In the bedroom, they both aim to please, and both benefit from the other's verbal affirmations—they can make each other feel beautiful, and both love to feel *seen* by the other. This is an intense one-night stand, but they'll learn a lot from their time together. If they decide to move in together, Libra should pick the neighborhood, and Virgo should plan the finer details of the move.

VIRGO & SCORPIO

Once Virgo digs up the herbs from the garden they were tending to, they take them to Scorpio's house, so they can use them in a spell they're casting. Is it a love spell? Maybe, but not for themselves. These two don't need a love spell to catch each other's eye. Their interest in each other forms without the help of special powders or potions.

Scorpio thinks Virgo is cool and admires their social connections, vision for the future, and ambition to help the world. Virgo is in love with Scorpio's mind, their ability to see through anyone, and their endeavor to find the deeper meaning in everything, from the arts to affairs of the heart.

Scorpio should show their artistic talents and try to be more flexible than they often are (they can be very stubborn!). In turn, Virgo would be wise to keep their criticisms to themself. Scorpio doesn't need to hear it. They struggle with a critical inner voice already and need a partner who is supportive by being reliable, calm, and kind, not by offering help in the form of criticism, constructive or otherwise.

Their energy in the bedroom is intense—everything is intense with these two—but also plenty of fun. Virgo is up for trying whatever kinky ideas Scorpio has. They can be great friends with benefits, and they're sure to grow very close as confidants. If they decide to commit and move in together, they should continue to schedule time to connect and not let their busy schedules keep them from spending time together.

VIRGO & SAGITTARIUS

There's certainly tension between these two, but they have so much respect for each other, as well. They're both adventurers. Sagittarius quests for truth by traveling around the world, reading books, and spreading their wisdom near and far, while Virgo journeys inside, looking for inner knowledge, and spreads their insights, skills, and knowledge to those they work with.

So, where does the tension come in? They have different communication styles—Sagittarius sometimes feels like Virgo is being sneaky (much to Virgo's dismay, because Virgo considers themself a very straightforward person), while Virgo thinks Sagittarius can be too bossy or demanding. They can get through this: Sagittarius should try not to jump to conclusions about Virgo—practice patience!

All that said, they do inspire each other. Virgo feels at home with philosophical Sagittarius, and Sagittarius is inspired by Virgo's productivity. If they can establish open and honest communication, these two can have a fantastic relationship. They have a great time partying together, too. Sagittarius's festive energy feels like home to Virgo. This union could be a fun and casual relationship. If they stick together and decide to move in, Virgo can expect to do more traveling, and Sagittarius can expect to learn the proper way to hang a roll of toilet paper (or whatever Virgo's particular needs are!). In the bedroom, Virgo's sensuality and Sagittarius's stamina make for hot evenings and passionate quickies early in the morning before work.

VIRGO & CAPRICORN

These two Earth signs are very busy: Can they make time for each other? Capricorn knows it's important to let off steam after a hard day's work. When you climb as many mountains as the sea goat does, you know a bit about pacing yourself. But as the sign of service, Virgo often works overtime, leaving their job and heading to another, or heading home to work on one of their many projects. Even their hobbies become sources of income eventually! Capricorn can't make Virgo take a break ... but Capricorn can remind Virgo, by the simple fact of their presence, that having a good time, enjoying life, and taking a break are some of the best ways to ensure that you stay productive. In fact, Capricorn is one of the signs Virgo is able to have the most fun with, because Capricorn really *gets* what a good time means to

Virgo: totally hedonistic, fleshy, physical, lusty, and sensual.

Their energy in bed is very compatible; they both enjoy role-play and bringing props into the bedroom—Capricorn loves their toys, and Virgo loves to see what Capricorn plans on doing with them (as well as using some toys themself, too, of course!).

Capricorn admires Virgo's intellect and their philosophical take on the world. These two would be wise to make some accommodations for each other—Virgo should show how nurturing they are and that they take initiative to get what they want. Capricorn should show Virgo that they can compromise and be flexible. If they decide to move in together, a cozy fireplace to curl up in front of as they unwind after their long days would be ideal.

VIRGO & AQUARIUS

If the world were organized and run by Virgo and Aquarius, things would *work*, and innovation and change would be in the air. Public health would improve and going to the post office might not even be such a pain. But they don't rule the world . . . not yet. In the meantime, they might want to make some time to romance each other. Aquarius admires Virgo's depth, but they can be overwhelmed by Virgo's constant criticism—Virgo can combat this by offering helpful solutions to Aquarius's complaints.

Spending time with Virgo means that Aquarius will need to confront their own fears and limitations. Virgo admires Aquarius's work ethic, as well as their intriguing mix of rebelliousness *and* dependability. Aquarius is cool, an out-of-the-box thinker, a rebel . . . but they're still someone Virgo can count on. Virgo learns a lot about boundaries, self-care, and good habits from Aquarius (or, if Aquarius happens to be going through

a harder time in their life and indulging in bad behaviors, Virgo will learn about self-care by seeing an example of what *not* to do!).

These two can make amazing things happen together; however, their combined energy is very intense and they will have to make adjustments in how they relate. Their energy in the bedroom is unlike any they've experienced with anyone else—they learn a lot about themselves and their needs through the intimacy they share. Air sign Aquarius has electric energy that mingles with Earth sign Virgo's grounded sensuality in a special and exciting way. If they move in together, Virgo should plan their meals, and Aquarius should pick out their appliances. These two signs are capable of fixing or building anything. Aquarius is a tinkerer and inventor, and Virgo is a worker and builder. They need to make sure they do not try to fix each other, and instead focus on building trust and intimacy.

VIRGO & PISCES

Pisces's magic is cast at night under the light of the Moon, during dreams and late-night parties, under the stars and the sea: this mystery tantalizes—and frustrates—Virgo. Virgo's magic? Oh yes, Pisces shouldn't be fooled into thinking that logical, practical, down-to-earth Virgo doesn't have magic. Virgo's magic is cast in the garden, with the help of the spirits of the plants, under the Sun—how clearly you can see under its illuminating rays. This magic isn't cast during a daydream, either—it's intentional, a sentence spoken with clarity and will, with bare feet in the dirt, connecting with the Earth. Virgo's magic is just what the sometimes paranoid Pisces needs to see the crystal-clear truth. These two make marvelous magic together, with Pisces the dreamer and Virgo the doer.

These two signs are opposites; they bring different skills to the table, and when they can share each other's gifts, they're able to accomplish great things—and enjoy great romances. They're both flexible people who value communication, but Virgo needs plenty of transparency from Pisces, and Pisces needs more sympathy and less criticism from Virgo.

Their energy in the bedroom is phenomenal—they're both givers, so as long as they communicate their needs, they'll be able to fulfill each other's desires. Virgo's earthy sensuality and Pisces's imagination come together for a fulfilling, romantic, and sexy coupling. They can be casual partners, as long as jealousy doesn't get in the way. If they decide to move in together, they can expect late-night heart-to-hearts and riveting conversations at the breakfast table.

LIBRA

THE SCALES

DATES: SEPTEMBER 23–OCTOBER 23

PLANETARY RULER: VENUS
ELEMENT: AIR
MODALITY: CARDINAL

PERSONALITY

The Sun sets on the horizon. The Moon shines brightly. It is the equinox, and there is equal day and night. The wheel has spun through the first half of the zodiac, and now a new perspective arrives as the wheel reaches the opposition of its starting point; a mirror is created, and Venus likes what's in view.

Libra is the only sign on the zodiac wheel that is symbolized by an inanimate object, the scales. Ruled by Venus, the planet of harmony, Libra aims to create balance through compromise and justice. An intellectual Air sign, Libra is a diplomat and also one of the most romantic signs in the zodiac. But Libra's life is not all love letters and parties (although that's a big part!), but instead is full of the destiny of learning how to compromise and weigh, as scales do, important decisions.

As a cardinal sign, it's the first sign of its season, autumn. Libra is an initiator, forward-thinking, and trendsetting. If you ever get in Libra's way, well, they'll probably hold the door open for you with a smile, but that doesn't mean they're not someone to watch out for! And if you fall in love with a Libra? Expect to learn a whole lot about relationships—they are *the* sign of partnership, having lived a life so focused on balancing with others.

AT THEIR BEST

Likely the most trendy, fashionable person you will ever meet, Libra isn't just artistically creative but is highly intelligent, as well. They have an incredibly sharp wit, allowing them to hold a conversation with anyone. They can flatter as well as build an argument—most Libras have considered law school at some point! They're logical and great at holding an objective view, and advocating for people is one of their strengths. They love to connect with others and can be fantastic matchmakers, too. Charming, social, and flirtatious, they know how to give a compliment. Considerate and willing to compromise, Libra is mindful of etiquette, yet still knows when to crack a naughty joke.

AT THEIR WORST

Always one to keep things in balance, they can be as brutally mean as they are sweetly kind. They love their lovers, but they also love having an archnemesis to gossip about or compete with. They're not indecisive per se, but they'll take a very long time to come to a decision, deliberating every option. If forced to come to a conclusion, they will say something that pleases the other person rather than the truth. Sometimes vain, snobby, and hooked on their cell phones and devices, they can be shallow, unreliable, and phony, charming their way out of a problem.

LOVE PERSONALITY

Ruled by sensual Venus, the planet of beauty and pleasure, Libra knows romance, but do they know love? They certainly yearn to. The immature Libra feels their life can't be complete until they've fallen in love. The wise Libra has learned that being in love doesn't "complete" anything. It just opens more doors: doors to healing, learning, journeying.

Libra is an excellent flirt, but their true talent is compromise. Sure, they can sweet-talk their way into someone's heart, but Libra's destiny is to learn how to employ their profound people skills in their relationships (not just in love, but business, family, and friendship, too), because it's not simply falling in love that makes you complete; it's having meaningful, supportive relationships that make life wonderful.

FIRST IMPRESSIONS

Likely the most stylish person you've ever met, Libra is attractive, easy to get along with, and difficult to forget. It's not just their good looks and charisma that leave an impression but also their sharp wit. They likely walked into the party fashionably late, and maybe you have caught their eye while they were taking off their coat. *Who are they?*

Libras are sharp dressers, usually wearing whatever is on trend, as well as a soon-to-be-fashionable accessory. They're generally very nice to everyone and often travel with a pack of friends, making it hard to read how they really feel about you. But that's part of their allure. Even though they're so chatty and outgoing, there's still this air of mystery, because the way they communicate when they first meet someone can be very polite or even aloof. What are they really thinking? They are charismatic, magnetic people, and when you spot one, it's hard not to be intrigued!

FLIRTING TECHNIQUES

You're in luck! Libra loves to flirt (that's why this section is so long), even if they're not that interested in you. Flirting with a Libra isn't hard—it's getting a date that is. So, how can you flirt with a Libra and leave an impression? You need to be *cool*—popular, trendy, in-the-know, witty, cultured, and doing something exciting with your time. Show that you're in charge of your life, that you're independent, a leader, and a person on the move.

Libra loves being pursued; however, if there isn't much of a challenge, they'll take your attention for granted. To keep Libra interested, be vague about whether or not you're interested—not in them (of course, they're wonderful!), but about whether or not you're interested in a relationship or looking for commitment. Libra loves talking about marriage, even if they have no interest in doing it themself. If an indecisive Libra thinks that "I don't know, I need to think about it" is a fine reply to say to everything from "What do you want for dinner?" to "Will you leave me in your will?," then it's a good enough answer for you to give, too, when they ask whether you're looking for a partner.

You can also spice things up by letting them know that someone hot has been talking to you—they like a little innocent competition! They also don't trust people who are totally single—honestly, what is wrong with you that you're alone? All that said, you really need to strike the perfect balance of giving attention while being unattainable and very cool. Libra loves to feel like they are playing hard to get even though they also love the thrill of the chase. Balance!

Libra is great at small talk, but that doesn't mean they are dumb: Libra loves analyzing people, learning about their

157

motivations, and talking about psychology. So ask them about why they think a mutual friend is acting so oddly, or about the secret motivation behind someone in the news. A little bit of gossip doesn't hurt as an icebreaker, either!

Once you're regularly texting with a Libra (which is likely to happen, as this sign has plenty to say and loves talking), be regular with your communications. This doesn't mean you need to be at their beck and call every time they contact you, but when they learn they can count on a "Hey, how's your day?" text in the afternoon, they'll grow to trust and feel comfortable with you.

DATING STYLE

Dinner and a movie are always fine with Libra—especially if the dinner is someplace new and exciting and the movie is an artsy film in a unique theater. Always be sure to compliment how they look, because half the fun of going on a date for Libra is getting dressed for the occasion! Group dates are also fine with Libra (notice how I said *fine* twice? Libra is amenable to most suggestions!). They're very social people who enjoy bouncing from friend to friend at a cocktail party to say hello (and show off their date!). A group photo with all their friends at the end of the night also fills them with joy. Chatty, social Libra loves to go from talking with you, to their bestie, and then to another cutie. But don't be alarmed by this! Libra just has a flirtatious personality and puts on the charm with everyone.

Libra is also very intelligent, and a date who puts their brains to use is a welcome change for them and their nonstop party agenda. If a "study date" is applicable to your situation, go for it! Or invite them to an exciting lecture, event at a museum, or trip to a historic location. Even the zoo or plane-tarium would work—Libra loves to learn.

RELATIONSHIP APPROACH

Libra learns early on in their love life that heartache stinks and that having a backup lover to flirt with when one disappoints or ditches you is a good way to pass the time (and avoid deal-ing with sadness). As Libra matures, they use relationships less as a distraction and more for fulfilling a natural human need: connection.

Libra is very comfortable in ethically nonmonogamous relationships, but monogamy suits them, too—Libra loves relationships, in whatever form they may come, as long as they can trust their partners. But Libra does have a possessive streak, so keep that in mind. In whatever type of relationship they may be in, it's important that they put themself first sometimes, as they have a tendency to forget about their needs because they're so involved in the lives of others.

Libra will bend over backward for you, so make sure to do the same for them. Classic romantic gestures can't hurt: flow-ers, a love letter, chocolates. Even better are acts of service to show Libra that you're thinking of their comfort. Pay for a cab ride home for them when they're working late and too exhausted to take public transportation. If they drive, wash the car for them so they don't have to.

Don't forget birthdays, anniversaries, and other special occasions. For Libra, part of the fun of being in a relationship is celebrating these events! They enjoy being surprised, so use one of these occasions to get them an unexpected gift.

SEX

Libra is delicate and gentle in many ways . . . in the bed is not one of the places you'll see this manifest, though! Sure, during foreplay there may (hopefully!) be plenty of dirty talk—they are an Air sign, after all. They'll play coy, especially because they love being pursued. They'll blush when you send a nude, but in bed, they're ready to fuck and be fucked, hard, by someone with strong hands and stamina. Pin them against the wall, and then have them straddle you.

Sex is an opportunity for logical, in-their-head Libra to get into their body. It's a chance for them to get grounded, physically and spiritually. Whether through sex or masturbation, the mind-body connection sex brings is massively heart-opening for Libra.

Set the mood by making sure the space is *beautiful.* Cleanliness is definitely important, so be sure to stuff the pile of dirty clothes you have out of sight in the closet. Get a large mirror and place it strategically near the bed, and crack a window or turn on the AC—Air signs need *air,* and sex can get quite steamy!

TURN-ONS

Libra is vain. They love taking selfies. So bring out a mirror for them to watch while you two have sex. Talk to them about how hot they looked the first time you saw them, and how hot they've looked every day since then.

The submissive Libra can be quite the spoiled, bratty princess, and they have been very, very bad. Do they need a spanking? The only sign in the zodiac not symbolized by a mythical being, animal, or human, Libra often loves to objectify or be objectified in the bedroom.

That said, when it comes to humiliation or degradation, be sure to thoroughly communicate about it beforehand, because Libra wants to feel like they're pleasing the person they're with and that they're doing a good job.

For the dominant Libra, teasing their partner with soft tools, such as ticklers and feathers, is likely to be a turn-on. Grooming and dressing their partners is also something that may appeal to the dominant Libra. Libra is accommodating in everyday life, but in the bedroom, dominant Libra gets off on calling all the shots!

TURN-OFFS

As much as Libra loves the chase, they value communication and are searching for it when with a new partner. So don't go MIA. Whether it's not getting a text from you all day long or a silent fuck, Libra will not be into it.

When their partner is unwilling to try toys or experiment in bed, Libra feels judged and bothered by it. Libra loves their gadgets, so welcome new toys in the bedroom! Libra dislikes close-minded people, and if they feel like you're trying to prevent them from having fun, they'll lose interest in you.

Be sure to pump up their ego. Libra can be self-doubting and overthink things. If they had a hard day at work, help them unwind with a massage.

LIBRA & ARIES

It is said that a Libra is just an Aries who went to charm school, but the funny thing is, when a Libra meets an Aries, they are usually very excited they have found someone they can be *real* with.

Libra is always charming no matter what, and Aries is always impressed by how charismatic they are. The main difference between Aries and Libra is that the ram can be thoughtlessly self-centered in a way that's truly confusing to Libra. However, if the ram has grown out of this less desirable part of themselves and is more mature, Libra will love how the ram really sticks up for the people they care about, going to battle to defend those they love.

In Aries, Libra finds a warrior who will advocate for them, and in Libra, Aries meets a partner who gives them space to be themself while still being the teammate they've been longing for.

One of Libra's favorite things about spending time with Aries is that they have an insight into them that other people seem to miss. Aries wants to be Libra's hero, but both signs sometimes have the ability to back out of a relationship quickly—Libra going off to flirt with someone else and Aries simply doing their own thing. If they're not totally ready to push things forward, they'll leave the other behind.

The energy in the bedroom is dynamic—Aries's fiery passion meets Libra's cool seduction. The union of Mars (Aries) and Venus (Libra) seems promised to be blessed by the heavens, making this a delicious hookup or a rewarding long-term relationship. If they choose to live together, Libra should decorate, and Aries should be mindful to help with the chores.

LIBRA & TAURUS

Both ruled by luxurious Venus, Libra and Taurus appreciate beauty and harmony, and generally have easygoing, gentle demeanors. There's a lot of sleeping, eating, and lazing with these two. Although Libra can't help but follow Taurus's lead, eventually Libra may get bored, leaving Taurus for a night out on the town, while Taurus texts them from the couch asking when they will be home.

Both Libra and Taurus enjoy being spoiled and spoiling the people they care about, but what's critical is that these two signs actually listen to what the other person wants instead of just giving gifts they wish to receive. Libra may gift Taurus with tickets to the opera, when really Taurus just wants a simple box of marzipan and a night in.

As easygoing as this pair is, if they stay together for longer than a fling, some intensity is sure to arise. Libra challenges Taurus to cut out their bad habits and to bring more balance into their life. Taurus also challenges Libra, forcing them to examine darker parts of their psyche and to confront fears, issues around intimacy, and getting their shit together financially. Libra will have to learn to process grief and open up to transformation. This relationship ends up being much more intense than the first few dates make it seem!

Their energy in bed is decadent. Their shared materialism and vanity is fun to explore with plenty of toys and mirrors in the bedroom. Libra adores being devoured by Taurus's eyes, and Taurus appreciates being doted on by considerate Libra.

If they choose to live together, ideally, it would be in a stately and ancient castle ... but in the middle of a busy city, where Libra can socialize and Taurus can be near good take-out.

LIBRA & GEMINI

In Libra, Gemini finally finds someone on their level in terms of being creative, a social butterfly, and able to have a good time. In Gemini, Libra finally meets their intellectual match, someone with whom they can have deep and relevant conversations.

But can a relationship between these two really be more than just fun and late-night phone calls? Bringing things to a deeper level emotionally can be difficult, as Gemini gives Libra too long of a leash, resulting in Libra not always being able to give Gemini the undivided attention they may want.

In turn, Libra may not have the guts to confront Gemini about how they're really feeling, leaving things in limbo—a mentally stimulating limbo, but a limbo nonetheless. If they can work out these issues, then the energy these two can create together is fantastic. But they'll hit other walls. Gemini may accuse Libra of not caring about the *right* issues and focusing on the wrong things, or straight up being shallow, while Libra will think Gemini is annoying and small-minded. Whether or not they're getting along, they'll have a lot to talk about.

This is a fantastic one-night stand, one where these two will blow off plenty of steam after a long day (or week, or year) of holding "it" together. Their energy is electric! Their communication styles are compatible, making it easy for them to express their desires, even though they are quite intuitive with one another. If they move in together, their home will be busy, with plenty of work being accomplished.

LIBRA & CANCER

Libra can be a show-off, and when they are on a date with Cancer, they can't help flaunting who they are out with, posting pictures to social media and taking them to places they can be seen. Unfortunately, Libra doesn't know that Cancer's favorite place is hiding in their shell. Well, lucky for Libra, this usually isn't enough to scare Cancer away, because in Libra, they find someone they can build a peaceful and harmonious home with—or at least someone fantastic and charming to shack up with for a weekend of casual sex!

If it's going to be more than a fling, it's important to note that neither Cancer nor Libra is great at handling confrontation, so they need to find ways to communicate with one another. Between Cancer's moodiness and Libra's tendency to sit with a decision for a long time, weighing all the options, there can be a lot of back and forth in this partnership.

They both act as if they don't care for drama, but they keep finding it in one another. If the relationship doesn't turn into something passive-aggressive, these two can manifest a caring, thoughtful partnership.

The tension between them certainly makes for very passionate sex: Cancer's intuition paired with Libra's communication skills combine to make for lovers who are able to explore a whole lot with each other.

Cancer is ruled by the Moon, and who doesn't enjoy staring up at its beauty? Libra, who is ruled by Venus, certainly does. But the Moon is changeable, which may stir insecurity in Libra. Cancer would be wise to show their loyalty to Libra, to keep their scales from quivering. And Libra, too, would be smart to display their serious side, as maturity is a very important quality to the crab.

LIBRA & LEO

These stylish signs have a lot in common: they love drama; they both want to be catered to; and they are both hard to impress. Leo, the sign of royalty, finds in Libra someone they can really talk to and whose judgment they can trust. In Leo, Libra finds someone who is just plain *cool* (despite being a Fire sign!), someone they're inspired by, someone they share the same hopes and dreams with.

Fire and Air (their elements) make for quite a storm in the bedroom. They should bring in the mirrors and cameras, for sure, but even before they reach the bedroom, building anticipation with long love letters and phone calls increases the passion for these two.

They build a solid social circle together and enjoy going on journeys, whether to an exotic location or just a road trip. These two are best friends, and it's this friendship that builds a strong connection between them, whether they are casual lovers or married. Their home should be large and spacious for all the parties they will throw together—it's unlikely these two will lead a quiet, boring life together. Leo's parties always turn into a wild scene, and social Libra has a hard time resisting the fun. If these two do end up walking down the aisle together, expect the most over-the-top ceremony you've ever seen—hand calligraphy invitations, dramatic floral displays, and riding down the aisle on horseback.

LIBRA & VIRGO

Even the most relationship-oriented Virgo can have a loner streak in them, and this causes concern for Libra, who finds Virgo to be one of the most puzzling people they have ever met—but also one of the most thoughtful!

Stylish, charming Libra can also stir up a bit of envy in Virgo. Virgo, who precedes Libra on the zodiac wheel and who is often portrayed as the maiden, can be seen as the awkward teen wearing braces, while Libra is the slightly older, much cooler, more experienced adult, who has long forgotten the questions on most preteens' minds. They're no longer wondering, "What's kissing like?" Libra knows exactly what kissing is like. So, you can see there is a bit of tension between these two signs, and likely some awkward bumps in the road. All that said, this can be a spiritually fulfilling union where they teach each other about material security and self-esteem.

As long as Libra is not too passive-aggressive and Virgo isn't too critical of Libra, things can work out well for them. Both signs enjoy catering to their lovers, and finally, with each other, they've met someone who is as thoughtful about decision making as they are. But these two need to make sure that they don't get stuck in endless rounds of "What do you want for dinner?" followed by "I don't know. What do you want?"

In the bedroom, they'll explore each other's wildest dreams. Virgo's lusty, earthy vibe and Libra's cool, seductive energy combine for an intense evening.

LIBRA & LIBRA

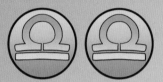

Finally! Someone who loves to flirt as much as they do. They'll instantly get along—but whether or not they still like each other after a few hours needs to be seen! If they don't become frenemies—or straight-out enemies—lots of romantic gestures fly between these two, including plenty of gift-giving and love letters. This pairing is perfect as a fling or something casual, and two Libras are likely to keep each other around as a person to flirt with when the need arises.

If these two decide to settle down with each other, they'll build an impressive home with plenty of space for entertaining. They'll enjoy a busy social life, as they both have so many friends and colleagues they enjoy keeping up with. Encouraging each other to be independent is one of the best ways to ensure success between these two. Jealousy may pop up because they are both so flirtatious; however, as long as

they keep an honest line of communication open, make it clear that they are each other's number one, and set firm boundaries, these two will do what they can to please their partner.

Ruled by gentle Venus, Libra needs to be with a partner who is straightforward and decisive. They're turned on by a strong-minded energy, so Libra would be wise to remember to take the lead at times, especially when it might not come naturally to them. Being able to ask for what they want is an important issue for both of them. Of course, it's a different story in bed—they're both very expressive about their needs there, and they're able to communicate with each other very bluntly about what they want! They'll enjoy experimenting together—their shared electricity could power one hundred vibrators! (And they actually might own that many, as they love tech!)

LIBRA & SCORPIO

Scorpio might be the most mysterious sign in the zodiac to many people; however, it is Libra whom Scorpio is bemused by. Libra also has complicated feelings about Scorpio. They'll either be envious or incredibly inspired by Scorpio's savvy, seductive abilities, and the wealth they're frequently able to amass.

Scorpio's mystical vibe inspires a lot of fantastical daydreams in Libra's mind, but because the scorpion can have a hard time reading Libra, Scorpio may intentionally make them jealous or do something dramatic that unintentionally pushes Libra even further away. Communication between these two won't always be easy, as they may both try to send subliminal messages without being straightforward about their desires. Libra is usually direct and a good communicator, but Scorpio's intensity may have them fearing a confrontation.

Building a solid friendship before moving into romance might be the best way to start—Scorpio needs to see that Libra won't flirt up a storm with everyone they meet (hard!), and Libra needs to know that Scorpio isn't using them for their time, money, contacts, or affection. Once they're able to develop a sense of rapport and humor with each other, many of these issues can be overcome. They certainly both love to gossip and enjoy dissecting people's motivations, so they'll have plenty to talk about on that front. Spiritual topics are sure to come up for discussion, too.

Scorpio is surprised by seemingly soft Libra's powerful presence in the bedroom, and Libra is also surprised by the tender romance the tough scorpion may show in bed. If they decide to live together, their home will be a blend of high-tech comforts and antique touches, with space for entertaining for Libra and plenty of privacy for Scorpio.

LIBRA & SAGITTARIUS

This match makes for one fantastic friendship—as long as Sagittarius is mindful that Libra's feelings can get hurt by their blunt behavior, and Libra can understand that their polite behavior may sometimes be misinterpreted by Sagittarius as phony. That said, Libra does get a chuckle out of Sagittarius having a little too much fun and saying something unexpected at the dinner table. They'll enjoy sharing intellectual pursuits, reading books together, and discussing current events. And they'll also enjoy sharing plenty of dirty text messages and sending nudes!

Something that Libra admires about Sagittarius is that they aim to do the right thing, even if they miss the mark sometimes. In turn, Sagittarius appreciates Libra's coolheaded, logical mind and passion for justice. Sagittarius thinks Libra is really something else: The flirtatious, ditzy, and sometimes superficial stereotype of Libra is something that Sagittarius just doesn't see. Sagittarius sees a person who tries to get along with everyone, enjoys all life has to offer, and takes serious matters seriously, giving them the time and respect they need to be dealt with delicately.

In the bedroom, Libra loves the physical energy Sagittarius brings, while Sagittarius is turned on by Libra's imagination. This is a fantastic fling but works very well in the long term, too. If they choose to move in together, they should live someplace with plenty of culture and things to do.

LIBRA & CAPRICORN

The first thing most people learn about Capricorn is that they're very driven, which means finding the ram in the office. This might frustrate a Libra, who may be concerned that their Capricorn crush won't have time to party with them, but they will be sorely mistaken. Capricorn definitely makes time to party, and they party even harder than Libra does, most of the time!

Libra would be happy to know that they are just the kind of person Capricorn would love to have on their arm at a business function. In fact, being around Libra and learning from them about how to be a better diplomat helps and pushes Capricorn even further in their career. These two make quite the power couple.

But Libra's lessons in the relationship land at home, not in the public sphere. In Capricorn, Libra finds someone they're able to build a home with, someone who creates a sense of grounded stability by how responsible they are. This person really feels like family to Libra.

Libra needs to learn to be patient, as Capricorn really takes their time before jumping into a relationship. Meanwhile, Libra's like, "Wake up, we are in a relationship!" All human connections are partnerships to Libra, you know. Capricorn may get annoyed by Libra's indecisive nature, while Libra may be hurt by Capricorn's pessimistic attitude. Libra is full of sweetness, but Capricorn is just too busy being real to be sugary. If they live together, Libra needs to give Capricorn plenty of space to complain and moan.

LIBRA & AQUARIUS

Aquarius's creativity catches Libra's eye. Libra has a thing for cool people, and it doesn't get any cooler than Aquarius. These two are both Air signs, and they find it easy to connect intellectually ... and sexually. Whatever kinky thing one is into, the other is up for trying out! The sexual chemistry between them is electric.

That said, there can be bumps in the road regarding communication, as Aquarius can be a bit of a loner, forgetting to check their phone while they spend time in the studio or riding their bike. And Libra likes to keep up-to-date with what's happening with their lover.

Aquarius is totally in awe of Libra's smarts, how cultured and often how well traveled they are. If Libra needs any help catching Aquarius's attention, they should know that showing off more, and being their own unique selves, won't hurt—Aquarius is attracted to people who are unafraid to stand out.

No one can build an argument like Libra can, and while Libra is certainly one of the sweetest signs, in Libra, Aquarius sees someone they want on their side should they need backup. Aquarius would be wise to make sure their Libra lover feels like they are in Libra's corner, too, should they need help sticking up for themself. If they live together, they might find that Aquarius does a little more lazing around the house, even though they are both very social people.

Libra is ruled by the lovely planet Venus, while Aquarius's planets are a little colder, a little stranger: serious Saturn and rebellious Uranus. It's an odd combination of energies at first glance; however, when you combine a strong sense of responsibility and a dash of eccentricity with kindness, diplomacy, and love, it's a recipe for an exciting and steadfast relationship.

LIBRA & PISCES

Libra takes time making decisions, weighing right and wrong, choosing the just option. Pisces swims in circles, seeing all sides to a decision . . . and sometimes taking both courses of action. These two signs will either learn a tremendous amount from each other or it will be an awkward mess.

In Pisces, Libra meets someone who inspires massive creativity within them, and who also inspires them to get their act together about health and wellness. Some of Libra's most healing connections may be with sensitive Pisces; however, the worst hangover in Libra's life may well be with a Pisces who encourages them to indulge too much. In Libra, Pisces meets someone they can face their greatest fears with—that is, of course, if Pisces is ready. Whether or not this union ends up being a nightmare or a partnership that leads to unimagined healing depends on where they are in their lives.

The energy in bed is imaginative, sensual, and often very intense. If it's just a fling, it's sure to have quite a long entry in both their diaries. If they stick together long term, they'll have to hammer out communication issues—Libra needs to speak in specifics with Pisces, a sign that can be all over the place, and Pisces has to be clear in stating their needs—but over time they'll be surprised by how much more they have in common than they realize. These two are both social people who enjoy building connections with others, and if they live together, their home may be more of a place for entertaining than either of them would have imagined!

SCORPIO

THE SCORPION

DATES: OCTOBER 23–NOVEMBER 22

PLANETARY RULER:
MARS AND PLUTO
ELEMENT: WATER
MODALITY: FIXED

PERSONALITY

A fallen tree rots by a pond, decomposing . . . but life thrives in the decay. Small animals find shelter and food, and these tiny animals become food for bigger ones. The bigger ones die, and the cycle continues. All endings are beginnings. Scorpio knows this.

A psychic, emotional, and creative Water sign, Scorpio is a fixed sign, meaning they fall in the middle of a season—in this instance, autumn. The waters are still, like amniotic fluid protecting new life, which is being formed. There's a level of control to Scorpio, but also creativity.

Traditionally ruled by Mars, Scorpio knows that endings must take place. This sign's modern planetary ruler is Pluto—a transformation always follows an ending. And don't forget: Power. Both these planets have plenty of it, as does the little scorpion, whose intense sting is something to be cautious of.

AT THEIR BEST

Highly focused and determined, perceptive Scorpio gets what they want. A magnetic and sexual being who oozes power, Scorpio makes things happen. Major transformations take place thanks to their efforts. Patient, inquisitive, and analytical, they are superb researchers. Fantastic listeners, they know how to keep a secret and are happy to help you psychoanalyze the motives behind anyone you're having a problem with. A deep and meaningful conversation is only a phone call away when you can call Scorpio your friend.

AT THEIR WORST

As jealous, resentful, vengeful bridge burners who aren't afraid to embarrass, bankrupt, or ruin themself (or you), for Scorpio the ends justify the means, especially if you've fucked them over. Paranoid, they're often in crisis mode, responding to any perceived threat with hypersensitivity, and lashing out. Forget about defensive—the scorpion can be straight up offensive. This sign is very secretive, and you may never know the truth about how they feel; alternatively, you could sit down for a seemingly innocent coffee date only to be thoroughly criticized, called out, and put down. As cool as they can come across, they do get overwhelmed by their emotions. For every manipulative Scorpio out there, there's one that's gullible, willing to believe anything that confirms their ideas about themself and the world.

LOVE PERSONALITY

Scorpio is no stranger to intense emotions. They're not afraid of falling in love . . . but they do sometimes question their own lovability. Life has not always been easy for the scorpion, but intimacy, sex, and close relationships (both sexual and platonic) make the difficult times worth fighting for.

Scorpio dwells in dangerous places—if not always literally, then emotionally. They're familiar with the landscape of "rock bottom." They've been there a few times, you see, as they've gone through many transformations in their life, ultimately being reborn like the phoenix. Scorpio has seen some shit—and they just can't relate to someone who has had it easy or who hasn't known loss.

They crave depth in their relationships, and above all—whether or not they realize it—Scorpio needs to be with someone who can stay *present*, someone who can stay grounded and provide security while Scorpio wrestles with their tendency for catastrophic thinking and obsessions, someone who will be patient when they're feeling angry, envious, or resentful. Scorpio has a tendency to overanalyze and be cynical—not always an easy combination. They may see the worst in a situation (it's part of their defense mechanism) before being able to see the bright side.

Scorpio's partner needs a tough shell for the sting their scorpion will sometimes deliver. Scorpio is looking for someone who will take them seriously when they are upset, but also be able to lift the mood when Scorpio's dark side creeps in. Scorpios love to love, and they love to fuck, but there's a slim chance they'll love *you*. Scorpio is very discriminating about who they let in, but when they do, expect to be loved as deeply as anyone could. Think matching tattoos, vials of blood for your anniversary, a crypt reserved for two.

FIRST IMPRESSIONS

These mysterious, sexy people hold intense eye contact and have strong poker faces. You'll leave your first encounter less concerned with what you thought of them and more anxious about what they thought of you. What exactly were they thinking when they looked you up and down, you'll wonder. Your Scorpio crush will likely be wearing all black, but don't be alarmed if they greet you in something more unexpected—antique mourning jewelry, leather, fishnet stockings, sequins, studs, and even chains find their way into the scorpion's wardrobe.

Scorpios exude power . . . unless they feel like hiding. If you encounter them online, their photos will either be exquisitely shot by an exceptional photographer with the best equipment, lighting, hair, and makeup, or they will be layered with several hundred dark filters, obscuring their face for total privacy. They're one of the few people who can look good when photographed from below. Rarely will you see a sweet, smiling candid photo of Scorpio floating around . . . if you do, trust that they were up to something!

FLIRTING TECHNIQUES

Ask them what they plan to dress up as for Halloween. Even if it's April, most Scorpios enjoy talking about their party plans. Halloween, a holiday that's part of Scorpio's season, was originally devoted to honoring the dead. Now it's one of the only days Americans wear lingerie in public! Sex and death are so deeply entwined, and all Scorpios know this!

Flattery goes a long way with Scorpio. Will they be suspicious of your random compliment? Probably. But Scorpio's ego can always use a boost, and if you're going to keep the compliments coming, they'll keep you around for at least a little while.

Scorpio isn't into small talk, but they're also unlikely to share their deepest secrets with you on your first (or even fifth) meeting. Open up about yourself. Don't share something too vulnerable (you don't want to come across as stupid to Scorpio), but something personal enough to show that you've got depth.

Even the most skeptical Scorpio secretly believes in magic; tell them you read your horoscope and that it said you would connect with a crush today. When flirting and complimenting Scorpio, don't make it too obvious that you're talking about them when you say, for example, that you love a certain smell that clearly is part of the profile of the fragrance they wear . . . but don't imply that you aren't. Scorpio loves having a mystery to solve, so leave them wondering whether you're talking about them!

All that said, don't be at their beck and call, or else they'll lose respect for you. Give them a compliment, share a secret, and then leave them with some mystery. Don't answer their text right away if you're busy at work or relaxing. Win your Scorpio over by proving that you have a life, and more importantly, self-control. It will be all the juicier for them to make you beg for it in the bedroom.

DATING STYLE

Take the scorpion out for a date at a restaurant with a private dining room, as Scorpio is big on privacy. For a more casual date, a stroll through a graveyard with deep, stimulating conversation is a good move. For a night in, binge-watching true crime, fantasy, or horror movies is always a fine idea.

The mysteries of life and death are intriguing to Scorpio, the detective of the zodiac, and Scorpio's keen research abilities are unmatched (so, if you cheat, expect them to find out!). Intrigued by the occult and fascinated by psychology, Scorpio wants to know what makes people tick, spiritually and emotionally. Going to a panel or lecture together about one of these topics is a great idea.

Scorpio isn't into PDA . . . usually. However, in more intimate environments, like a house party or after hours at a nightclub, they are typically up for some strip poker, spin the bottle, truth or dare, or an orgy.

RELATIONSHIP APPROACH

Reliability is important to Scorpio. In a polyamorous relationship, it's important to schedule time with them, so they know that they can depend on you. Not just for "date nights," but also for the "crying, laughing, cleaning out the garage, or impromptu trip nights." These are just as important to Scorpio because part of why they want to be in a relationship is for the support—it's really not just about sex and shared secrets for them. In a monogamous relationship, this is just as true. You need to *be there*. Flaky, flighty, moody people leave Scorpio feeling totally drained. No matter what sort of relationship they are in, being mindful about jealousy, obsessive behavior, and power struggles is also important.

Scorpio needs a partner who is down-to-earth and doesn't start drama just for the fun of it. Life is hard enough, and a relationship should be an emotionally safe space for all involved.

Financial stability is also very important to Scorpio. Scorpio would be just as upset to find a partner who isn't generous or is shady about cash and lies about their financial situation as they would to find that their loved one flirted with the enemy. In fact, Scorpio would almost rather you flirt with their enemy because then they could have a fun time getting back at you by flirting with *your* best friend. Scorpio gets very (VERY!) jealous, indeed, but they also fear being used, lied to, or led on.

They enjoy having a partner they can create things with: art, music, a business. Scorpio is a sign that knows two heads are better than one—just like two bank accounts are fatter than one. When people come together and combine their talents and resources, amazing things can happen.

SEX

Everyone's heard about sexy Scorpio, the most alluring sign in the zodiac. Their reputation seems like a lot to live up to, but they don't have a hard time keeping up with it at all!

To Scorpio, sex is a merging of souls, a powerfully spiritual experience. They are intense lovers, very passionate, and they put every inch of their being into their lovemaking. During masturbation, the union they achieve with their inner truth is one that's healing and often is an important part of their spiritual practice, too.

Scorpio typically loves kink, and will likely have a few books about BDSM, S&M, or fetishes in their library, as well as a whole trunk filled with toys. Scorpio is intense, and kinky sex can lead to altered states of consciousness and psychological benefits for them. Even a scorpion who doesn't necessarily want to *do* anything kinky in bed will usually enjoy talking about kinks, and will at least likely be up for exploring yours by attending workshops together, going shopping for sex toys, or just listening to your stories about whatever it is you're interested in. If you are more "vanilla" in bed than Scorpio, be sure not to kink-shame them.

When you're setting the scene for sex with Scorpio, be sure to bring plenty of drama to the bedroom: silk or velvet sheets, expensive lingerie, a roaring fireplace, and some mirrors on the ceiling.

TURN-ONS

Tell them the dirtiest thing that you're into. Even if it's not especially dirty, letting them think that you're too embarrassed to tell anyone else about it and that they're the only one you can trust to give this information to is a major turn-on for them! They love feeling powerful and important, and they love a partner who isn't afraid to be kinky.

Any kind of role-play that highlights a power dynamic or that requires lines like "I shouldn't be doing this to you, but . . . " is a turn-on. Being bad feels good to a Scorpio! Being ruled by Mars, Scorpio may want to explore impact play (think paddles, whips, spanking), and being ruled by Pluto, Scorpio finds any kind of control in bed a turn-on. Role-playing where you pretend to be strangers will appeal to Scorpio: Any fantasy that includes mystery will get them going. Scorpio is very imaginative, and this quality shines in the bedroom—they'll be up for pretty much any scene and will have an easy time taking it anywhere.

Scorpios are extreme people, and that extends to the bedroom—but that doesn't necessarily mean they *want* to take control in bed. The submissive Scorpio will enjoy feeling totally used by their partner. Scorpio, in everyday life, is very emotional, but the dominant Scorpio may swing to the other extreme—the cold, hard master who takes no shit from their sub!

In group sex scenarios, Scorpio wants the extreme—all holes filled. Scorpio is very visual, too, so while blindfolds are fun for sensory play (which they do enjoy), they'll likely want to rip them off after a while so they can watch your body connect with their own.

Each sign rules a body part, and Scorpio rules the genitals (as well as the excretory system—I'll let your imagination take that from here). Worship their genitals or have them worship yours! Mutual masturbation is also a fun way to heat things up in the bedroom. Sex is very psychological to Scorpio, so describe to them what you see them doing in detail, and explain how it makes you feel.

This has been a very raunchy chapter—but know this about Scorpio: Sex is a spiritual act for them. Being with a partner who is present is their biggest turn-on.

TURN-OFFS

As I created the outline for this book with my apprentice, they asked incredulously, "Scorpios have turn-offs?" I didn't know how to answer them—it's true, not much turns the scorpion off! But there are a few things: Kink-shaming a Scorpio is certainly a bad idea. Bad kissing is a no-no—be in control of what's happening with your mouth, as a sloppy tongue will gross them out.

Privacy-conscious Scorpio is also going to be cautious about filming a sex tape together, so if this is something that really turns you on, approach this idea mindfully.

SCORPIO & ARIES

Aries's rambunctious and confident presence is very different from enigmatic Scorpio's cool vibe, and these two might have some awkward adjusting to do. Aries will push Scorpio to break some of their bad habits, and Scorpio will test Aries to face their fears. But these two have more in common than one would think. They're both intense, and they like that about each other—Aries forcefully expresses what Scorpio sometimes wishes they could scream out loud, and Scorpio is strategic and savvy in ways that make Aries swoon. These two could take over the world together . . . but could they fall in love?

Yes, Aries's go-getter attitude as well as their sincerity makes Scorpio feel safe—Scorpio can trust that Aries isn't bullshitting them, because Aries clearly doesn't have the patience to.

For Aries, Scorpio is someone they can explore sex with—and the fireworks are huge between these two. The energy in the bedroom is fiery and passion-ate. They are both ruled by Mars, a penetrating, energetic, warrior planet, and the intensity shared between them is palpable.

These two need to be sure to keep their tempers in check. Both of these signs can be too intense for something casual, but if they are able to manage something that's just a friends-with-benefits situation, you can bet they'll hit up a sex party or some kind of kinky workshop together fre-quently. If they choose to live together, a hot tub and a fireplace are good ideas to help them unwind after long days being in charge and taking over the world.

SCORPIO & TAURUS

Scorpio and Taurus are opposites on the zodiac wheel, and they usually chuckle when they realize the difference between their seasons—one arrives when the flowers are blooming; the other, when dead leaves need to be raked from the ground. Their energies are so different, but in many ways, they give each other exactly what they need.

Scorpio needs someone down-to-earth and reliable, sensual and creative—Taurus is a perfect fit. And Taurus needs someone who can help them transform during times of change, who is as savvy and street-smart as they are sexy—Scorpio certainly fits the bill. Their communication styles are complementary, which certainly helps, too.

So, what's to keep this union from being a perfect match made in the stars? They both need to be mature, and it helps if their kinks or desires in the bedroom align. Scorpio also can't try to manipulate, trick, or lead Taurus on, unless they want to lose them forever, and Taurus needs to be mindful about giving Scorpio too much grief.

In the bedroom, Taurus's stamina meets Scorpio's potent, passionate sexual energy—the vibe is sure to be luscious and hedonistic. If they choose to stick together and decide to move in, their home will be a cozy one. Taurus should be the one to shop for comfortable furniture, and Scorpio should pick out the safes for all the valuables they are sure to amass together!

SCORPIO & GEMINI

Can anyone outsmart Scorpio? Yes, Gemini can. But this is a book about love compatibility, so why should we even worry about who could outsmart who when we're all just trying to make love here? That's what defensive Scorpio needs to remind themself of when they're looking at Gemini as a potential match—as someone to have fun with, not someone who potentially could beat them at their own mind games. Yes, Scorpio, *fun*. Gemini wonders if they've heard of it . . . although they really do admire Scorpio's work ethic, inspiring Gemini to kick bad habits and get their shit together.

Scorpio is very intuitive, but when they're bolstered by Gemini's witty, sharp mind, they find a friend who is a phenomenal sounding board. Scorpio would be wise to be a little less defensive around Gemini. However, the truth is, Gemini does stir insecurity in this sign. Being around the twins forces Scorpio to realize that they've got to

make some changes and that it's time to face their fears. It would be best if Scorpio remembered this: On their way to taking over the world, it might be wise to have someone on their team who could outsmart them. It would only make them even stronger!

When connecting with Scorpio, Gemini would be wise to tap into their inner artist and their luxurious side, and Scorpio should show how intellectual and well traveled they are to impress witty Gemini.

In bed, Gemini's versatility and Scorpio's passion make for a powerful combination. This could be an intense one-night stand, and if they're in it for the long haul, they'll be surprised at how they're both able to keep things fresh. If they live together, their home will be a high-tech haven (surprisingly, Scorpio's touch), but with room for an herb garden (again surprisingly, Gemini's).

SCORPIO & CANCER

These two are some of the most private people you'll ever meet, yet together, they come out of their shell: Cancer inspires Scorpio to see the world, to learn new things, and to go on adventures, and Scorpio ignites passion in Cancer, inspiring them to pursue their creative endeavors and to let loose and have a good time. Of course, they still like their privacy, too. They have a lot to do behind closed doors! Their energy in bed is hugely passionate—Scorpio shows Cancer things they never thought possible, and Cancer delivers the emotional intensity Scorpio craves.

Cancer should show how dependable they can be—Scorpio *understands* Cancer's moods, but Cancer's sometimes hot and cold behavior still worries them. Scorpio adores watching the phases of the Moon change, but until they really understand their crab lover, Cancer retreating for space may stir insecurity in Scorpio. Scorpio has some things to be mindful of, too: Cancer craves a partner who is grounded and down-to-earth. Both of these signs are emotional, so they need to learn to be solid rocks for one another if this is going to be more than just a very sexy fling.

A friends-with-benefits situation could be great if they don't have major jealousy issues they are working with. Although these two sometimes enjoy a little jealousy play, both parties must be emotionally healthy and be communicative with one another for this to work successfully. If they move in together, their ideal home would be one with a secret address—these two signs both crave privacy! A gated community works, too, or a magnificent castle shrouded in fog on a far-flung island— Cancer will have a marvelous time making it a home, and Scorpio loves the drama of a hush-hush locale. It depends on the budget, of course. A room in their house that is behind a secret bookshelf door will do if the castle hasn't come into their possession yet!

SCORPIO & LEO

Plenty of drama is in store for these two powerhouses! Mysterious Scorpio isn't comfortable with the spotlight the way Leo is—but they could get used to it! Scorpio admires Leo's creativity and their ability to be in the public eye. Even though Scorpio is very private, they understand that success means having your name out there—and what better partner to have on your arm while the paparazzi take your photo than glamorous Leo? Leo feels at home with Scorpio in a way that's special and unique. Deep, emotional Scorpio is someone Leo can share their child-hood pain with, someone they can talk to about their past—and past lives (Scorpio is into that kind of thing!)—and with whom they feel they can build a solid foundation for the future.

They're very different, but some-times that kind of tension makes for an even sexier atmosphere. The drama Leo brings to the bedroom turns Scor-pio on; they're both signs that need sweaty, sexy passion. Leo would be wise to show their royal side and their ability to keep a secret. To capture Leo's heart, Scorpio should show their sensitive and emotional side and their ability to keep a very cool head under pressure. Scorpio is savvy and street-smart, something Leo can appreciate. They can expect over-the-top theatrics if this is just a weekend fling. If they decide to stick it out and live together, Scorpio needs to remember to give dramatic and romantic gifts as well as plenty of compliments to Leo, and Leo needs to give Scorpio a balance of space and close affection. Their home is their place to recharge, so they need space as well as affection.

SCORPIO & VIRGO

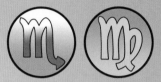

Virgo is the sign that rules the digestive system, and Scorpio rules the excretory system—that about sums up how well these two work together. If you're not one of these two signs, this probably doesn't make sense to you, but I promise you that when Virgo and Scorpio read this about themselves, there will be a quietly sighed, enlightened *ohhh* . . . These two are a great team.

Virgo's grounded energy and cool demeanor feel safe to Scorpio, while Scorpio's ability to see beneath the surface is inspiring to Virgo, who is in love with the scorpion's mind. These two are best friends who understand each other . . . until Virgo starts to criticize too much and Scorpio starts lashing out while under stress. Kindness is key to making this relationship work! And neither sign is known for being an ass kisser. That just means that

when they do get along, it's sincere and genuine, which is something they both appreciate.

The energy in the bedroom is a blend of Virgo's sensual and lusty vibe and Scorpio's kinky, intense nature. They can be friends who hook up casually, but if they decide to live together, they'll see another side to one another. Scorpio will get a deeper glimpse of the fantasies Virgo has about their future, and Virgo will gain a deeper understanding of Scorpio's creative process, as well as how they recharge after emotionally intense days. Scorpio would be wise to show their mystical side to Virgo (as down-to-earth as Virgo is, they do appreciate that in a partner—if only to have intellectual discussions about *why* they're interested in such things), and Virgo should display how determined and dependable they are.

SCORPIO & LIBRA

My teacher, astrologer Anne Ortelee, taught me that the archetype of Libra is all about the date: the choice in restaurant, the conversation at the table, the polite part of romance that's in public. But the archetype of Scorpio, which is the sign after Libra, is all about the part *after* the date: Will one of them invite the other in for coffee? Will they go upstairs? Will the lights turn off? Will things escalate? Will the two, who treated each other so sweetly at dinner, become one? Now, we're not talking about archetypes; we're talking about real people who both care about the date and whatever comes after. But it's important to remember this general difference between their energies—Libra first focuses on how they'll get along intellectually, while Scorpio first concentrates on how much they'll share emotionally.

They'd be wise to slow down a bit and enjoy the process. Although very social, Libra needs to schedule time with Scorpio to slow down and unwind, instead of hitting up each party during the weekend. Scorpio would be smart to demonstrate to Libra how brave they can be, and how they stick up for their friends.

So, what will happen on the date? Scorpio might hint at how mysterious they find Libra—although, as Scorpio often does, they may not totally say it straightforwardly. They are a mystery themself, and Libra will have plenty of questions to ask Scorpio about their values and will likely be curious about Scorpio's many talents and how they acquired them. In the bedroom? They're sure to surprise each other—they should both check their expectations at the door. This is an intense fling! If they stick together and decide to move in, their space will be filled with plenty of antiques *and* high-tech touches.

SCORPIO & SCORPIO

When two Scorpios meet, so much magic can be made . . . literally, because these two are often into the occult! But the magic also occurs between the sheets, where they both have a deep need for emotional connection, as well as passionate, dramatic sparks. And the magic also occurs on a bench by the river—they like to be near their element, water—where they can quietly people watch or share stories about their lives. Neither of their lives has been easy, but with each other, they can find someone who understands.

They both have a straightforward way of communicating but are very strategic about when they reveal their information. They're both very psychic, too, so many conversations may be held nonverbally—but, hopefully, all will be held *in person*. These two can be as paranoid as they are psychic, so entire arguments may play out in each other's heads after receiving a poorly composed text message with no lighthearted emoji, and a period punctuating the end of a sentence. Did they send such a cold and final text on purpose? They endlessly wonder about each other's motives. They have to be honest and talk before paranoia builds up too much.

When they have fun, they like to go all out—sex parties and drinking, or, if they're over that phase of their lives, peaceful meditation retreats at stunning scenic locations. They're both craving stability from a partner and need to be with someone who can stay present in the moment. At home, they both desire space and a cool, airy setting where they can calm down after emotionally exhausting days. Intimacy is important to them both, and again, communication is the key that will get them there. Hopefully, they don't sting each other first.

SCORPIO & SAGITTARIUS

These two probably met at a bar—even a sober Scorpio likes to spend time in shadowy places, and a sober Sagittarius, too, can't resist a pool table or a dartboard. Scorpio wonders: Is it luck? Does Sagittarius hang out at the bar all day? No, Sagittarius is too busy traveling, reading, and living to spend time in a bar all day! Scorpio meets Sagittarius, sees how talented they are, and is either jealous of them, wants to be them, wants to screw them, or all three. Sagittarius meets Scorpio, and often doesn't know what to make of them! Sagittarius has heard of the enigmatic Scorpio, but *could it be true?* Sagittarius wonders, *Am I just like everyone else, thinking Scorpio is a total mystery?* You see, Sagittarius is smarter than most people, so they've just got to crack the Scorpio case and get to know them better!

The best thing these two have in common is their desire to explore—Scorpio usually leaning toward hidden places, while the scenes Sagittarius is attracted to are more bustling. But their shared desire for gaining wisdom and understanding is something that makes this partnership flourish. If Sagittarius can show how artistic and sensual they can be, Scorpio will be even more turned on, while Scorpio should reveal to Sagittarius their light and easy side that enjoys socializing. If these two have good communication about their needs in the bedroom, this can be a very hot coupling thanks to Sagittarius's fire and Scorpio's passion. If they move in together, their shared altar space is sure to be a peaceful one—they both have a spiritual side.

SCORPIO & CAPRICORN

Scorpio's ruling planets are Mars and Pluto, and Capricorn's is Saturn. Without launching into a whole astrology lesson, trust me when I say these are intense planets. Mars battles, Pluto destroys, Saturn imposes limitations . . . yet, somehow, these two have so much fun together! Perhaps it's because they both have strategic minds and they enjoy plotting schemes together. But, more likely, it has to do with the energy in the bedroom: usually very kinky, always very sexy. These two have solid communication, which helps them out a whole lot as a couple.

To Capricorn, there is no one cooler than Scorpio, and to Scorpio, Capricorn's brain is a major turn-on. They both have a passion for things that are old, antique, historical, haunted, and time tested. They enjoy watching horror movies together, but also have a guilty pleasure of watching romances and tearjerkers—nothing gives Scorpio more glee than seeing if they can make Capricorn get emotional over something sappy (it's very hard to do, which makes it even more rewarding for Scorpio).

They need to watch out for jealousy, and they need to keep the lines of communication open, instead of riding on how easy things feel "at first" and assuming things will always be just fine. Scorpio would be wise to reveal their nurturing side to Capricorn and to be patient with Capricorn about how and when they express their emotions. Capricorn would be wise to slow down a bit and learn to relax. If they move in together, it will be into an old mansion that might house a few ghosts—Capricorn secretly hopes there's treasure hidden in the walls, and Scorpio is itching for a séance.

SCORPIO & AQUARIUS

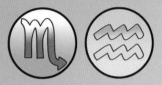

Do these two have anything in common? It would seem not, between the intense and emotional scorpion and the detached and logical water bearer, but both of these signs know that there's always more than meets the eye, and that you always need to look beneath the surface to *really* grasp a situation.

These two make a fantastic detective team—Aquarius has the gadgets, and Scorpio has the interrogation skills—but this book isn't meant to be about career paths for the signs. That said, Aquarius very much admires Scorpio's work ethic and drive for success, seeing the scorpion as a powerful person in their field and hoping to achieve the same for themselves, too. Scorpio's affection lies more in the private, personal realm (as it always does for the emotional scorpion), looking to

Aquarius as a solid partner and friend with whom they can build a foundation and a future.

There is a lot of tension between these two and the energy in the bedroom is very intense, as Aquarius's cool energy clashes with Scorpio's heat. They can both overthink things, but Scorpio will count on Aquarius to be the one they lean on when their mind is going a mile a minute. Neither of them is a stranger to sadness, but Aquarius will lean on Scorpio for some wisdom and a pep talk, and they need to be able to provide this support to each other if they want things to work out for more than a fling. If they move in together, Aquarius will be surprised by how handy Scorpio is around the home, and Scorpio will be surprised to see how indulgent Aquarius can be!

SCORPIO & PISCES

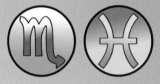

These two enigmatic Water signs are a mystery to many, but to each other, they feel comfortable—they're in their element! Emotion, intuition, and imagination are the realm they live in, which is great when they're being creative, but not so great when paranoia arises. These two need to build trust if the relationship will work. Scorpio adores Pisces's creative abilities and the fun times Pisces shows them (they know where all the best parties are). And Pisces admires Scorpio's mind, looking up to them for wisdom when they need inspiration or someone to lean on.

But Scorpio needs to be mindful that their ambition could be read as ruthless to Pisces, who may wonder if Scorpio is trampling other people on their way to the top. Scorpio would be wise to show that they indeed care about helping others and not just themself. Scorpio is far more decisive than Pisces, which can lead to frustration. Pisces should not be too wishy-washy, as Scorpio needs a dependable partner they can lean on, someone who will be by their side when the going gets rough, not hiding under the bed out of fear.

They have plenty of passion in the bedroom; they both have active imaginations, and their psychic connection in bed is phenomenal. This is a fantastic hookup, and if they want to be together long term, they need to patiently build a friendship. If they move in together, continuing to have thoughtful discussions about boundaries is key.

SAGITTARIUS

THE ARCHER

DATES: NOVEMBER 22–DECEMBER 21

PLANETARY RULER: JUPITER
ELEMENT: FIRE
MODALITY: MUTABLE

PERSONALITY

An archer nocks their arrow onto their bowstring. A moving target off in the distance is struck. The shot seemed impossible . . . but luck seems to follow Sagittarius wherever they go.

Of course, it's easy to be lucky when you've got the ability, the smarts, and the energy to put yourself in the right place at the right time. Ruled by the planet of abundance, Jupiter, Sagittarius is an optimist, open-minded to all possibilities. As a mutable sign, meaning their sign falls at the end of a season— in their case, autumn—Sagittarius is curious, a philosopher and communicator who is committed to learning and sharing information. Armed with knowledge and eager to take chances, Sagittarius always seems to have good fortune come their way. Above all, Sagittarius is a seeker—of knowledge, pleasure, spiritual growth, and, of course, love.

AT THEIR BEST

Cultured and well traveled, broad-minded Sagittarius values tolerance, honesty, and knowledge. Positive thinkers, these optimistic, festive people are filled with gratitude for the good things they've been blessed with and the things they've worked hard for. Uninhibited and bighearted Sagittarius seizes life, thinks large, and stays on the go. Adventurous and spontaneous, they are visionaries, deep thinkers, and spiritual, and have a fantastic sense of humor.

AT THEIR WORST

Sanctimonious Sagittarius rides a very high horse and is one of the rowdiest partiers you'll ever meet. They say all the wrong things, at the worst times, and being as blunt as they are gets them into trouble. Prone to exaggeration and carelessness, they can be reckless and impatient, as well as impulsive, pretentious, arrogant, and inconsiderate. The know-it-all Sag can come across as holier than thou.

LOVE PERSONALITY

Sagittarius wants to run free—but that doesn't mean they always want to run free *alone*. This adventurer certainly goes on solo missions, but having someone to share the journey with is definitely something they desire. They just need someone who can keep up. They're attracted to witty people who share their thirst for knowledge—and their occasional need to have a rowdy, fun time. Sagittarius might be half human, half horse, but really, they are half nerd, half party animal, and they're attracted to people who satisfy both needs.

Sagittarius believes in love at first sight and wants a partner who can be their best friend. Don't ever try to "tie down" a Sagittarius, but know that if they love you, this loyal Fire sign will always try to do right by their partner. While a Sagittarius can sometimes be a rule breaker, that doesn't mean they don't deeply care about doing the right thing. They approach love like they approach all things: optimistically, full of life, and with an open heart.

FIRST IMPRESSIONS

Sagittarius may have been partying when you first laid eyes on them—their boisterous laugh is infectious. There is, however, a very studious side to them, too, so it is just as possible that you met them in the school library, studying away. Or, perhaps you first met them on an airplane, on their way to their next adventure.

Sagittarius has eclectic taste when it comes to fashion, often wearing items they've picked up on their many journeys. They love shopping, and they're just as generous with the people around them as they are with themself. Sagittarius doesn't dwell on scarcity—they see the plenty in the world, everywhere.

Charismatic and a great storyteller, Sagittarius surely has something exciting to tell you as soon as they meet you. They are natural salespeople, and by the time they're done talking about whatever it is they are excited about, you'll be a believer, too.

Sagittarius has fantastic aim, so it's likely that whatever your first impression is of them, it's the one they wanted you to have, whether the archer is looking for love or any other kind of relationship. They're also very blunt, and their straightforwardness can be either refreshing or a turn-off!

Imagine a holiday dinner: Friends and family gather around a massive feast, everyone gives thanks before digging in, drinking wine, laughing (someone might be crying, too), giving each other gifts, and telling personal stories (some that may be slightly exaggerated). That's Sagittarius's energy.

FLIRTING TECHNIQUES

It's easy to be enamored by Sagittarius—they're so smart, and they love to have fun. Sagittarius is attracted to social and spontaneous people who are intellectually curious, so in order to attract the archer, show how confident and adventurous you are.

It's a cliché icebreaker, but it works with Sag: ask them where they could go if they could take a trip anywhere in the world. Discussing spirituality is also a great way to get Sagittarius talking—even if they're an atheist, they'll have some passionate things to say about the subject.

Ask them about politics, their favorite book, or how they feel about a social issue. They are full of opinions, and they love sharing them. Asking someone questions about themself is obviously a great way to connect—people love talking about themselves, after all—but Sagittarius is especially eager to share their ideas, and an open, listening, thoughtful ear is sure to put them in a good mood.

They are straightforward people, and they'll appreciate you being direct about your interests; however, it takes more than thinking they are hot to leave an impression on them. You see, most people see the sex appeal in Sagittarius, a sign that's never had a hard time getting someone's number in a bar or a swipe on a dating app, but not everyone can pique their interest intellectually, which is really how you get a Sagittarius to think you're someone special.

Just want a one-night stand? Be straightforward, and it's likely Sagittarius will completely rock your world for the evening. But if you're hoping to get to know them on a deeper level, you have to connect intellectually. There are two sides to Sagittarius, the Centaur archer: the bottom half that's hung like a horse and the top half, a human with a bow and arrow. They can mount anyone and have a good time, but that's not enough to please the human side of them.

DATING STYLE

Sagittarius loves to travel and explore, so if you can swing a trip for two to an exciting city, do it! Sagittarius loves exploring other cultures, so however you can incorporate that into your date, try it. Don't plan too intense of an itinerary: Sagittarius likes to keep things flexible during a date.

If you're staying in, remember that Sagittarius loves to indulge: get a bottle of wine or some weed (if it's legal where you live), grab a massive bouquet, cook up a big dinner, and make sure there is dessert, too. Sagittarius craves one-on-one time; however, they're also very social, so if you invite some close friends to enjoy the meal with you, and then promptly kick them out after dinner for some lovemaking time, that will make Sag quite happy.

What else makes Sag happy? Shopping! Sagittarius gets a thrill out of consumption—of knowledge, booze, food, or consumerism. Take them someplace that has vintage pieces, antiques, jewelry, or games (they do have a very playful side).

Sagittarius also has a spiritual side, so go on a walking tour of places of worship, or go on a weekend silent retreat (just kidding—they can't keep their mouths shut, so a yoga retreat will do!), or visit a tarot card reader together. Even better, give each other tarot readings; Sag will enjoy the intimacy of discussing the images and meanings of the cards as you flip through the tarot book together.

RELATIONSHIP APPROACH

Get a passport, because being with a Sagittarius means seeing the world. Being with adventurous Sag also means you will need to keep an open mind. Sagittarius, despite a reputation for being a player, is one of the most loyal people, but they need space to do their own thing from time to time.

Don't try to control Sagittarius—they decide when and with whom they settle down, and settling down to them doesn't mean sitting quietly. They're still going to go on escapades, see the world, and enjoy life . . . you just get to do it all with them! They also want their partner to put in an equal amount of effort when it comes to "taking the lead." They don't want to be the only one setting up dates or making plans—both should be involved.

They are famously blunt, so you can expect them to be straightforward with you about settling down, marriage, children, and what they're looking for in their future.

Sagittarius lives life with the attitude "bigger is better" and "the more, the merrier," so they often are interested in open relationships or polyamory. They must learn, however, to schedule their time well and not make too many promises to too many people. They aim to keep their promises, they really do, but an immature Sag tends to say *Yes!* to everyone when they should really check their calendar first. Whatever sort of relationship they are in, they stand by the people they believe in until the very end.

Being with a Sagittarius means being on the receiving end of their brutal honesty. If you can't handle the truth, this isn't the sign to date.

SEX

Sagittarius wants to live life to the fullest, and that includes fucking. Sex should be big, loud, and passionate. But as fun loving as Sagittarius may be, there is a deeper side to them—one that you might not see if you just have a casual romp with a Sag (and they do have many!).

They crave safety and security in the bedroom, much more than they realize when they first begin having sex. Feeling protected and safe unlocks deep sexual fulfillment for them. Sex and masturbation are a big part of how they ground and center, how they strengthen their aura, and how they move through life while balancing all the emotions these adventurous people face on their journey.

Remember, "more is more" to Sagittarius. When you're setting the scene for lovemaking, don't just bring one bottle of wine—take them to a whole winery. Deck out the room in their element, Fire. Candles are fine, but a roaring fireplace is better. Fireworks in the night sky are best. An airplane bathroom works, too, if you two are fine with tight spaces. Fire signs thrive on drama and spontaneity!

TURN-ONS

Intellectual Sagittarius needs mental stimulation. Send them suggestive texts throughout the day, and then make them guess where to meet you after work—all that anticipation and puzzle solving will have them eager to take your clothes off.

They are size queens, and a fully charged vibrator should be kept in the bedroom at all times. They have fantastic stamina, so do your best to keep up with them! Their sign rules the hips and thighs, but having a nice backside is also a plus.

Massage them: oil them up, give them a deep tissue massage, and then begin teasing them sensually.

Group sex is great, gang bangs especially . . . if a huge party can't be arranged, being double teamed is quite fine, too.

The submissive Sagittarius runs free most of the day, so during sex, they might get off on the total opposite, being tied down or collared, snuggling up on your lap, purring like a domesticated cat. These are things that dominant Sag is into as well; they also enjoy scenes where they are the master, or even a cult leader.

Sagittarius gets off on love, so don't be surprised if they drunkenly proclaim their love for you while they orgasm, even if your hookup is clearly a one-time-only thing in a bar bathroom.

They are very physical, have lots of stamina, enjoy trying out new positions, and likely own a copy of the *Kama Sutra*.

TURN-OFFS

They're okay with a quickie, but if you can't pull any all-nighters or marathons (they'll stay in bed with you for days, getting up for brunch or a smoke, then hopping back into bed), you'll need to get with it.

Don't judge them for their past. Yes, it's not fair—Sagittarius is very judgmental—but past sexual encounters are not something they care to defend or explain to a new lover. It's in the past!

SAGITTARIUS & ARIES

Finally, someone who can keep up! Sagittarius has so much fun with the ram, and these two can party. Aries inspires Sagittarius creatively. Sag talks a big talk, but being around Aries inspires them to get things done. Aries has a lot of questions about life, and Sagittarius seems to know all the answers. These two can talk all day, and they prefer to do it in person, not over text. They can make something long distance work, but they want to be able to grab and kiss each other when the feeling takes them over.

In bed, the energy is passionate and carnal. These two likely told each other they loved each other on the first night, and even if that doesn't work out, they're likely to stay friends. These fiery signs can cause a big scene when they argue; however, they're just as prone to icing each other out, trying to prove that they're too cool for one another. Fortunately, they both know how to forgive and forget.

If they stick things out for the long run, these two will build a home filled with wild memories and hopefully a hot tub on the back porch, a glam touch for these two Fire signs who love to hang out nude together.

SAGITTARIUS & TAURUS

Oh, does Sagittarius think they know adventure? They should hear about the journey a sleepy Taurus went on from the couch to the fridge one morning at 3 a.m. It was really something! Taurus thought they saw a random cat, but it was just a shadow, and the cake they thought was still in the fridge had already been eaten a few hours earlier. Unbelievable! Silliness aside, these two have more in common than one might expect.

Taurus knows a lot about art and culture—things Sagittarius adores—so they will have plenty to talk about. Sagittarius is a pretty easygoing person; however, their energy is very intense to Taurus, which can be either overwhelming or very inspiring for the bull.

Being around Sagittarius, Taurus finds they need to confront fears and make changes—not something easy for this often stubborn sign to do, but change sometimes is necessary, and who better to do it with than Sagittarius, who believes that all things are possible?

Earth sign Taurus's grounding energy helps Sagittarius develop a routine for themselves, teaching them the importance of practice and ritual in their lives. The energy in the bedroom is intense—Taurus's slow sensuality collides with Sagittarius's stamina and fire. Their home will be filled with delicious and expensive things, but if Sagittarius sits on the couch as frequently as Taurus does, they'll get in a bad mood.

SAGITTARIUS & GEMINI

These two are opposites on the zodiac wheel, but they have so much in common: both value communication and knowledge and love to have a good time. Their differences? Gemini cares more about their place in the social scene, while Sagittarius doesn't care who they might offend during a rowdy night out on the town. When they argue, it's often over semantics (due to literal Gemini) or theoreticals (meta-phorical Sagittarius) and whether or not to look at the big picture or the details. Things can get bad quickly if they start lying to each other—if their relationship isn't built on respect and honesty, it won't work. However, they'll probably still hook up even after they call the relationship off! Old habits die hard.

When they get along, these adventurers are the best of friends who know all the most interesting people, visit the coolest places, and stay on the move. A long-distance relationship between these two can work, since they're both so willing to travel to see each other—not just in their hometowns, but anywhere in-between—and because of their communication skills.

The energy in bed is electric—they know just what to say to each other to turn each other on, and they both have the stamina and versatility to keep things interesting. If they live together, honestly, they'll hardly be home. For them, home is with each other, whether that's in a hotel, a tent on the beach, a spaceship, or their dreams.

SAGITTARIUS & CANCER

Sagittarius is a seeker...could Cancer have the answers? Water sign Cancer's spiritual presence is inspiring to Sagittarius; they want to know what the crab knows, and they can tell that being with Cancer will have them undergoing amazing transformations—although the process can be scary or uncomfortable. Fortunately, Fire sign Sagittarius is brave, something Cancer deeply admires about them. Cancer also admires Sagittarius's flexibility and stamina; it inspires them to get to work, create, and get organized and healthy, too. Sagittarius needs to go on walks to cool their head sometimes, also a good option for the crab, who might retreat to their bedroom with the shades drawn when a breath of fresh air and some sunshine might be better for them.

Sagittarius is ruled by Jupiter, the planet of growth and expansion.

Cancer is ruled by the Moon, which knows a thing or two about growth, but also of loss, as the Moon moves from full to new. Should Cancer worry that when their lunar phase is shrinking, they'll lose Sag's interest? No, because Sagittarius sees growth everywhere. The Moon may be changing shape, but the night sky grows around it, filling up the space that once was. Growth is everywhere. And while these two may have growing pains and some awkward moments, the learning process they go through together is deep.

The energy in bed is lusty, and they explore kinkier sides to their sex life. If they choose to live together, their home will be a cozy one with plenty of room for entertaining, and perhaps a telescope in the window to explore the landscape of the Moon. Sag would love to go there one day together and bring lunar Cancer home.

SAGITTARIUS & LEO

As Fire signs, these two have a lot in common: a strong sense of loyalty, big, generous hearts, and plenty of passion. But Leo can be stubborn and fixed in their ways while Sagittarius keeps an open mind; however, Sagittarius doesn't always know when to keep their mouth shut, whereas Leo has typically mastered this ability. Yes, Leo loves drama, but they know that there is strength and wisdom in silence, and Sagittarius is seeking wisdom.

Could Leo teach Sag a thing or two? They certainly could! And that's precisely why Sagittarius loves them: for their mind, their sense of adventure, and their faith. Sagittarius wants to learn, and Leo has plenty of wisdom to impart, so as long as Leo inspires and doesn't condescend, these two can stay up for hours talking ... or partying.

Sagittarius knows just how to show Leo a good time, and Sag's sense of adventure and ability to always know where the party is are things Leo adores.

If they choose to live together, spirituality is sure to be part of their lives. Soundproofing their home is also a good idea, as two Fire signs in bed are noisy—neither wants to hold back! Living far away from their neighbors is also a good option; however, living in the middle of nowhere probably isn't the best idea, as Leo and Sagittarius both love to be near where things are happening—museums, shows, restaurants. Short term, this is a fantastic fling; however, if Sagittarius isn't planning on sticking around, they better tell Leo before the party begins, not when they're putting their clothes back on.

SAGITTARIUS & VIRGO

Virgo understands that all we ever need to know about the universe and its mysteries is inside us. But Sagittarius still thinks it would be nice if we could type all that information up in books and share it with each other. Whatever ideas Virgo has, Sagittarius, a fantastic salesperson, is ready to sell them. These two inspire each other to act, making this an exciting union.

They both value communication, occasionally need their own space, and enjoy taking off all their clothes. Sagittarius is enamored by Virgo's earthy, sensual energy, and Virgo is impressed by the drama Sagittarius brings to the bedroom. Virgo is minimalist, but that doesn't mean they don't want excitement from their partners.

Virgo can worry quite a bit, too, so spending time with optimistic Sagittarius certainly lifts their spirits. Sagittarius feels very much like home to Virgo, but Sagittarius would be wise to tap into their artistic side, not just the intellectual, even though their mental connection is likely what brought them together.

Virgo would be wise to show how playful they can be—Sagittarius needs someone with a good sense of humor, as well as someone who they can play pool, chess, or Scrabble with on a rainy night. Although Virgo's go-to on a rainy day is just getting more work done on their side project, this is still something that inspires Sagittarius.

SAGITTARIUS & LIBRA

These two are busy: between all the dinners and social events, the shopping and traveling, the long nights on the phone gossiping, and the evenings spent at lectures, Sagittarius and Libra have lots to do. Sagittarius admires the trendsetting Libra, as well as Libra's logical mind. Justice is very important to both of them. Libra admires Sagittarius's curiosity and adventurous nature. Libra is extremely intelligent—you hear them gossiping and talking about petty things so often only because it's hard for them to find someone on their intellectual level—and Sagittarius, finally, is someone they can talk to.

Of course, there is the chance that Libra will find Sagittarius too extreme in their ways, too loud and obnoxious. And there is a chance that Sagittarius will think Libra is snobby or acts like they are too cool. But generally, these two are best friends. And not only do they love flirting with each other, but they also love to flirt with everyone else in the room—and they typically give each other enough space to do just that!

These two both love a good time, so the vibe in the bedroom is sure to be playful, sexy, and indulgent. They're fantastic friends with benefits, and their smooth communication style means that they can stick together for a long time, too. If they move in together, Sagittarius will learn how serious and focused playful Libra can be when they're at home, and Libra will get an insider's look at Sagittarius's creative process.

SAGITTARIUS & SCORPIO

Sagittarius has always had a crush on Scorpio, but for once in their life, wasn't sure how to say hi. Sag is unusually shy around the scorpion! Scorpio is certainly one of the most enigmatic and mysterious signs in the zodiac, and no one feels this more than Sagittarius. Good, Scorpio thinks! How happy they are to know they are able to get people under their spell, especially such a confident and intelligent person as Sagittarius.

But, truth be told, confidence is something Scorpio sometimes lacks. You see, no one is that obsessed with power if they feel totally secure in themself. Scorpio has certainly had a lot of rough patches in life. Sagittarius's confidence and "anything is possible attitude" are fantastic influences on Scorpio, as long as Sag has the patience and listening skills to relate to brooding Scorpio. Scorpio, too, will have to try to meet Sagittarius halfway on decisions, to compromise, and be as honest with them as Sag is with everyone.

Sagittarius will stomp off if Scorpio proves to be untrustworthy. Even if Scorpio doesn't *lie* to Sagittarius per se, Scorpio has the ability to put a mask on in front of strangers and hide their true self in a way that Sagittarius just can't—and it kind of worries Sag. *What are they really feeling? How could they switch from one set of mannerisms to another so quickly? What's the truth?* they wonder. It would be smart of Scorpio to clue Sagittarius in about their complicated emotions *before* they go to that meeting or party, so that Sag isn't caught off guard by it.

The energy in the bedroom is intense, and in Sagittarius, Scorpio will find someone who has the stamina to make all their wildest dreams come true. Anything kinky Sag might be curious to try, Scorpio will most likely be game for as well. If they live together, their home will certainly have a few books on everything supernatural, from alien encounters to stories about near-death experiences.

SAGITTARIUS & SAGITTARIUS

Two Sagittarius lovers together is . . . a lot. It's a lot of love, a lot of fun, a lot of partying, a lot of wisdom, but sometimes, a lot of less desirable things, too. For this to work out as anything more than a fling, each Sagittarius will need to learn some lessons about moderation, or else they'll max out their credit cards and end up in rehab together faster than you can say, *Another round, please!*

They've both been on many journeys and have so much wisdom to share with each other. If it's true that "the couple that prays together, stays together," then two Sagittarius hearts have a very good chance of lasting a lifetime, but a short fling is fun, too. Sagittarius doesn't place value on the quantity of time they spend with

someone, but the quality. A bright flame that dies out quickly isn't meaningless or petty to them.

If they live together, their home is sure to have a well-stocked liquor cabinet and a collection of beautiful glass pipes. These two are escapists, and while they typically like to hop on a flight to get away from things, when they are home, they have other ways of journeying than on the physical plane—the astral works just as well. If they're sober, a room for meditation is a must.

What about their bedroom? It's painted red, with plenty of candles everywhere. They're very active people, and there's likely a sex swing hanging next to the treadmill. They have sex on both—don't ask me how.

SAGITTARIUS & CAPRICORN

Both of these signs think they're realistic, but the truth is, Sagittarius exaggerates a bit, and Capricorn's pessimism weighs them down more than they need. Together, these two can keep each other in check—or totally annoy each other. Capricorn needs to try to keep it light every once in a while; miserably complaining too much is something Sagittarius finds totally unproductive (and they might say this to Capricorn, who will respond in shock that anyone could call them unpro- ductive!). Sagittarius would be wise to share their emotions with Capricorn, instead of over-intellectualizing things.

One thing is for sure: They both know how to have fun. Sagittarius thinks they're the wildest partier in the zodiac; however, Sag has a thing or two to learn about letting loose from Capricorn, a sign whose debauchery is unmatched despite how conservative and hardworking they can be in everyday life. They also work very hard for the things they believe in. They can get a lot done with each other, as Sagittarius offers unexpected nuggets of wisdom to Capricorn and helps them see things they might usually miss, and Capricorn teaches Sag about cash and, on a deeper level, about self-worth.

When Sagittarius's fiery passion meets Capricorn's lusty sensual energy in bed, a magical experience arrives for them both, as Capricorn feels comfort- able exploring all their secret desires with Sagittarius, and Sagittarius finds a partner in Capricorn who helps them really slow down and connect with their body. If they live together, Capricorn should let Sagittarius decorate, but would be wise to control the budget.

SAGITTARIUS & AQUARIUS

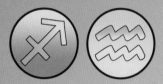

Aquarius appreciates people who aren't afraid to be themselves, so Sagittarius is definitely going to catch their eye. These two signs are best friends; both value communication and try to look at the world with a critical eye *and* a sense of humor.

Aquarius is certainly more fixed in their ways than Sag is, and has an icier sense of humor, but their vibe still works... usually. At least until Aquarius fact-checks something outrageous Sagittarius says, embarrassing Sag. Then they might have an awkward moment.

But, in general, these two are friends who love to get high, watch movies about aliens, and then hold each other tightly, paranoid about whether or not they might get abducted—although a small part of them is curious about the experience. You see, Sagittarius longs to explore distant lands and whole new worlds, while Aquarius never really felt like they belonged here on Earth. They wonder if they're really from a star system, far, far away, where the beings are highly evolved, valuing unity, intelligence, and kindness.

Aquarius ought to demonstrate how popular they are to Sagittarius, if they want to impress them, while Sagittarius shouldn't be shy about showing off. Sagittarius adores Aquarius's sharp, logical mind, and Aquarius loves Sag's fire and passion. In bed, the energy is electric—whatever Aquarius is in the mood for, Sagittarius can supply. This is a great fling, or a physical friendship, or a long-term relationship. Their intellectual connection keeps them strong. If they choose to live together, their home is sure to be a comfortable zone for lounging after long days adventuring.

SAGITTARIUS & PISCES

When psychonaut Pisces meets world traveler Sagittarius, they have plenty of things to talk about. Both ruled by Jupiter, the planet of growth and abundance, they're learning lessons in life about knowledge and faith—and Pisces can help Sagittarius listen to their inner voice more, while Sagittarius can help Pisces read through an instruction manual for once.

They admire each other's depth and respect each other's flexible, open-minded way of being. Pisces would be wise to tap into the social butterfly within them to attract Sagittarius, while Sag should show how patient and wise they can be. No, patience doesn't come easily to Sagittarius, but a mature Sag knows the right time to shoot their arrow, and that sort of mindfulness is very attractive to Pisces. Pisces feels like home to Sagittarius, a sign that's often on the road, while Pisces looks to Sagittarius for inspiration around their professional goals.

These two can make a great team, although there is some tension between them. Pisces can get so emotional, and Sagittarius can get so on their high horse, that frustration can happen. Hopefully, they can be kind to each other when these issues flare up, instead of ignoring or flaking on one another. These two need to keep their vices in check as well.

Their sexual energy is intense, bringing out unexpected emotions within each other. If they choose to live together, Pisces will intuitively know just how to set up the home in a way that's comfortable for both of them.

CAPRICORN

THE SEA GOAT

DATES: DECEMBER 21–JANUARY 20

PLANETARY RULER: SATURN
ELEMENT: EARTH
MODALITY: CARDINAL

PERSONALITY

Ascending from the depths of the ocean, traveling across the shores and up the steepest mountain, Capricorn finds their home at the top. They've seen it all—the dangers in the waters, the joy and physical test of the climb, and the cool, perceptive clarity the high peaks provide. At the top of the mountain, the sea goat looks across the land and notices that the grids of city streets are neatly organized and accessible, not over-whelming as they were at the base of the mountain.

Ruled by Saturn, the planet of time and limits, Capricorn knows that putting time into something will pay off—but is also acutely aware of the limited time that we have here on Earth. The melancholy born of this realization of the fleeting nature of life is profound in this old soul. As a cardinal sign, the first sign of the season—in this case, winter—Capricorn is an initi-ator and a go-getter, and as the last Earth sign, Capricorn is highly focused on building and growing.

AT THEIR BEST

Having overcome many obstacles, Capricorn is wise and experienced, understands the importance of responsibility, and empathizes with people who have seen great hardship. Ambitious and self-motivated, Capricorn is tenacious and achieves any goal they set their sights on. Business-minded Capricorn appreciates the past and honors tradition, while wisely planning for the future. Capricorn is not all work and no play, though; they "work hard and party hard," as the saying goes. Their dry humor is one of a kind, and they know how to have a good time.

AT THEIR WORST

Capricorns are very hard on themselves; they have difficulty being satisfied with their successes, feel overwhelmed by how to achieve more, and fear failure—and they can also be very hard on the people around them. They can be power-hungry, status-obsessed, opportunistic workaholics. Everything is a transaction to them. Rigid and cold, Capricorn can also be condescending, mean-spirited, and greedy.

LOVE PERSONALITY

In love, Capricorn reveals a soft, poetic side—separate from the hardworking or tough demeanor they often show. But they won't idealistically "wish" that things will work out as they gaze at shooting stars: you must prove yourself to be a caring partner by your actions, not just your words. Capricorn is looking for someone who is both tough and nurturing, some-one who has a sense of humor but also a deep sensitivity. In a relationship, Capricorn wants a partner who will make them feel cared for in a way that they can't provide for themself: Capricorn can make all the money in the world, but a touch from someone who will be there through thick and thin isn't included in their hard-won job's benefits plan.

Melancholy Capricorn has been called "cold" many times. This may lead you to believe that they are not romantic. They are! They're just very no-bullshit people. They'll flirt for fun and fuck because it feels good, but time is a valuable resource, and they're not going to waste it with just anyone.

Capricorn has also been called "rigid" or "controlling," but they don't try to control love. They know that falling in love is a force of nature that you can't make happen—or prevent from happening.

FIRST IMPRESSIONS

If you meet your Capricorn at work, you might admire their work ethic but worry that they're boring—the reverse is true if you meet them at a party! You'll wonder how they could possibly wake up to get anything done after all the hard party-ing you witness them partaking in. Certainly, Capricorn is one of the hardest workers in the zodiac, but when they let loose, it's often a scene.

No matter where you meet Capricorn, you'll find they're focused, well spoken, and usually well dressed. They can be materialistic, which often means they have nice clothes, and they prefer natural fibers to synthetic ones. Capricorn is a mystical creature, and as such, even the most somber-seeming sea goat has some otherworldly flair to them. They often come across as quite serious, but their devilish smile makes an appearance every now and then!

FLIRTING TECHNIQUES

Capricorn was usually too uptight in middle school to pass notes, but they loosen up as they age, and having a note passed to them at a party asking, *Do you like me?*, with check boxes for *yes* and *no*, will make them giddy.

Capricorn hates wasting time, so they're typically very straightforward about what they want. They do a lot in their everyday lives, so they often enjoy being chased; however, if you come on too strong, too fast, they'll wonder whether you just fall in love with anyone!

Online dating typically isn't exciting to Capricorn, as they value real-world experiences over virtual ones, but if you happen across one, don't waste their time, reschedule dates, or, worse, flake. They won't forgive you!

DATING STYLE

Stoic Capricorn is unfussy in most areas of their life; however, fresh flowers, fancy dinners, and cuddles on silk sheets are absolutely up their alley. They love to indulge during dates, whether it's with good wine, some weed, delicious food, or anything else. Taking a Capricorn shopping on your dime is never a bad idea. Just don't behave too foolishly with money!

Capricorn is very tactile. Show that you're good with your hands: make them pottery, or give them a massage. Take your Capricorn crush to old places, like a landmark building with rich history or a museum.

Spend time outside enjoying nature's wonders—if there's a remarkable natural formation near you, take them to see it. If they invite you to a work function, be on your best behavior. Read up on their field, and dress to impress!

RELATIONSHIP APPROACH

A Capricorn is rarely confused about what they want in a relationship. If they are, you can trust that they will schedule a time to get back to you later after they do some computations. Capricorn may be ruled by Saturn, a planet that's all about commitment, but they are totally cool with casual sex. They are ruled by the Devil card in the tarot, after all.

Capricorn is also thought of as being quite traditional; however, their respect for maintaining the strategies that have worked for them in the past doesn't mean they're not willing to try new things. Just because their parents or grandparents were monogamous doesn't mean they won't be open to polyamory. Their mature and responsible nature is perfectly suited for ethical non-monogamy, too.

In a long-term relationship, Capricorn is often eager to build a lasting legacy. Why else are they working so hard? They know they can't take it all with them in the end. They are looking for a future and a home with someone, even if there are no plans for marriage. A promise ring is typical—Capricorn loves gifts, and the opportunity to buy each other something beautiful and well made to symbolize their love is something they enjoy.

Have a goal, have a job, have a ten-year plan—bonus if your retirement plan is in order. Capricorn works their ass off, so one thing they really value in a partner is someone who is domestic and can help them build a warm home, which is something they've always wanted but often lacked throughout their life. Help keep them physically and emotionally nurtured, with good food and a sympathetic, trustworthy ear.

Rushing, pressing, or pushing them are all bad ideas, Capricorn must do things at their pace. Impatience turns them off—as does tardiness. Bad listeners make Capricorn feel unimportant; they want to feel seen by the people they care about. Irresponsible, unreliable, and flaky people who aren't mindful about how they budget their time, money, or energy lose Capricorn's interest quickly!

SEX

Turn off all outside distractions when you're in bed with Capricorn. Put your phone on airplane mode and encourage that they do, too. They can be hooked on checking their notifications, but they'll be super annoyed if they feel like you're staying connected with the outside world while you're supposed to be cuddling with them!

Life is hard, and if anyone knows it, it is Capricorn. Sex, with a partner or masturbation, is a heart-opening experience for them, one that elevates them from the pains of everyday life—it's when the heart opens that the most proactive shifts can take place. It recharges them, mentally, emotionally, physically, and spiritually.

Massage and energy work are great ways to set the mood before bed. Capricorn is very physical (they are an Earth sign, after all), so lots of hugs, cuddles, squeezes, and kisses are important. Capricorn is typically kinky, so hit up a sex shop together and see what appeals to you both. Role-play is usually up their alley, too.

TURN-ONS

Capricorn is *busy*, but they might have time to squeeze you in for a quickie. However, what they really enjoy is being able to forget about time while they are fucking. They want to get lost in a sea of each other's bodies. They want to taste, look, smell, and grab.

Positions that allow them to be fully embraced are perfect. They are totally open to experimenting, but to them, sex should be comfy, so keep that in mind the next time you

227

suggest the bathtub or the kitchen table. Supportive sex furniture is a good investment for this sign that rules the knees.

Bring the massage oil, but please, nothing with strange chemicals—Capricorn isn't into artificial flavors. They'd rather eat real whipped cream off your butt than get some strange synthetic in their mouth.

Rope bondage, collars, chains, and handcuffs are right up kinky Capricorn's alley. Slave-and-master scenes turn them on, as does teacher and student, or daddy or mommy delivering a spanking. They probably have a dungeon somewhere in their home. Both dominant and submissive Capricorns are very physical in bed and both get off on control and humiliation.

They love costumes and playing dress-up—getting theatrical in bed is totally something they're into. Leather, latex, or even lace and other textures in bed are lovely, too. Their sex toys are high end, but their taste in porn is often homemade videos of other lusty, in-love couples living out their dirtiest fantasies.

They typically take charge in group scenarios (they are a cardinal sign, after all), and enjoy weekend-long sex marathons with a partner or at a sex party, ideally in a luxurious mansion at an enviable address.

TURN-OFFS

Being closed-minded about sex toys or any accessory Capricorn wants to bring into the bedroom is a no-no; Capricorns love their stuff. You don't need to use their sex swing if you don't want to, but don't make them take it down, either. What do you think they're at work earning all that cash for? Also, don't try to boss around a Capricorn unless it's during consensual power play.

Capricorn can deal with a lot of bratty whining as well as genuine tears in bed—they get that sex is messy, emotionally as well as physically. But don't fake your emotions. Don't pretend to be happy when you're not, pretend to love them when you don't, or pretend to be indifferent when you are head over heels. Be real.

On that note: Slide into bed wearing a polyester robe and doused in a synthetic perfume if you want to turn your Capricorn lover off. Fake feelings are a no, and so are fake fabrics or scents. Fake nails? Fake hair? Fake teeth? That's all good, just don't smell like chemicals or fake your feelings.

CAPRICORN & ARIES

Time plays a crucial role in the love story of the ram and the sea goat. It's more than Capricorn's "five-year plan" or Aries's "two-minute attention span"; these two manage to weave a long history, running into each other over decades. Not that they mind. Sure, they might have gotten into a fight in the past, but time changes people. And anyway, these two highly physical signs are extremely compatible in the bedroom, so even if it's just for "one more night," they can't resist each other's touch.

Aries's thoughtlessness hurts Capricorn, and Capricorn's impossible standards hurt Aries. It's said that a Capricorn is just a grown-up Aries, but it's also said that Capricorn ages in reverse. A lot of mixed messages here! Will there ever be a right time for these two? Can they get along? Indeed, they will need to be careful not to be so hot (Mars, Aries's planet) and cold (Saturn, Capricorn's) together. It can work if they consciously try

to be gentler (looking at you, Aries!) and forgiving (that's for you, Capricorn!) of each other. Aries would be wise to show their intuitive abilities and protective nature to Capricorn. Capricorn *adores* having Aries at their side, helping defend them from whatever storms may come their way. And Aries loves Capricorn's logical way of approaching things.

If they stick together, these two can really be a power couple: Aries is a grounding energy for Capricorn to be around, and Capricorn inspires Aries to push further in their career. Their home is cozy yet busy, and they'll certainly have to work out a schedule of who should cook and clean—or hire help, because neither of these signs particularly wants to deal with chores at home! Aries should at least pretend to like to cook, or maybe bake Capricorn some cookies every once in a while. But if Aries goes through the trouble, Capricorn should praise them—Aries loves to be told they're the best!

CAPRICORN & TAURUS

There is an inner turmoil in Capricorn, pushing them ever further toward the limits of greatness. Capricorn knows sadness, defeat, triumph, and mastery. For a sign that is often called "cold," they sure have experienced plenty of emotions. So what happens when the sea goat meets one of the most chill signs in the zodiac, Taurus?

If Capricorn is a volcano, exploding into a new landmass, then Taurus is a mountain, unmoving. Taurus's ability to be in the moment, present, and peaceful is something Capricorn is unused to. Taurus's energy is either deeply grounding or else irritating to Capricorn's need to get going. There's an ease between them, but Capricorn isn't used to ease, and may distrust it or simply be bored by it. The antidote, then, is for Taurus to talk about the things that they are passionate about and ready to fight and protect. This way, Capricorn knows that their lover isn't just lounging in the hammock all day, doing crosswords, while Capricorn is running the world. Capricorn has some changes to make, too—Taurus needs a partner who will show their emotions, so Capricorn needs to be available to discuss feelings with Taurus.

Both signs appreciate material goods, though Taurus may have a harder time not spending money. Taurus sees Capricorn as worldly, cultured, and wise, while Capricorn sees Taurus as someone hugely creative, a fun person to party with. Taurus typically has wonderful taste in food, so that's something they should certainly share with Capricorn. In bed, the chemistry is fantastic: this pair can fuck for hours. If they live together, these two Earth signs are sure to have a home that's warm and energetic—a cozy fireplace to curl up in front of is a must.

CAPRICORN & GEMINI

While on the surface they seem to be an unlikely pair—and yes, their first meetings may be awkward—Capricorn and Gemini can be a fantastic match when true love's arrow hits.

Capricorn loves that Gemini keeps themself busy with interesting, intellectual pursuits. Gemini, a highly logical sign, feels comforted by Capricorn's cool ability to sort through complicated emotions and handle difficult issues. Gemini sees the little devil in Capricorn, and Capricorn sees the trickster in Gemini—they're a team to watch out for.

They take each other's time and energy seriously—for the most part. They need to be mindful about being punctual and not poking fun at each other's expense too much. Capricorn can't help cracking some jokes, and Gemini needs to try not to take everything too literally or seriously. I know, it's strange to have to tell Gemini not to be too serious when a Capricorn is also present, but, as either of these signs

will tell you, life is strange. They both do care about being polite, knowing etiquette, and following the rules . . . but they also know all the loopholes.

Capricorn is absolutely delighted by Gemini's energetic approach to lovemaking, and Capricorn has a certain something Gemini can't put their finger on that excites them so much. Sex with Capricorn is a transformative experience for Gemini—they leave their past notions about lovemaking behind. And Capricorn learns some cool tricks, too—not just in the bedroom, but in general, learning a lot through their relationship with Gemini about maintaining their emotional, physical, and spiritual health.

Long term, if these two live together, Gemini needs to understand that the home is Capricorn's safe space to scream into a pillow. And Capricorn needs to let Gemini turn the kitchen table into a workstation—at least temporarily, until they can get a bigger house, which we all know these two will work hard to achieve.

CAPRICORN & CANCER

Being at the right place at the right time is crucial for these two. When Cancer's circus comes to town, Capricorn may be clocking in late hours at work. When Capricorn's debauchery is under way, Cancer may be recovering in their shell.

When the two finally meet, somewhere between Cancer's side-walking step and the sea goat's ascent up the metaphorical mountain, they see in each other a kindred spirit, a rival, a best friend (and sometimes frenemy), and a lover. It's rare these two will feel indifferent about each other. But it is crucial that they make time for each other, and that they indulge in romance if that's where their hearts lie.

The energy in bed is dramatic—light, airy touches followed by intense passion. It's theatrical—it might even

be recorded! They both love role-play and are sure to engage in many scenes together. This is a hot one-night stand or a hookup that happens whenever one is in the other's town.

Their communication styles are compatible, a blend of practical and intuitive. Cancer sometimes goes into their shell, disappearing from the world, so they must be clear with Capricorn about their departure, as Capricorn is not one to be left in the dark about people they're supposedly intimate with. Living together will certainly be a test: peace and harmony in the home are crucial to Cancer; however, Capricorn needs to be able to tell off the neighbors if they feel it's the only path to peace (things work easier sometimes when you know who the boss is).

CAPRICORN & LEO

So similar, yet so different, Capricorn and Leo are regal signs indeed; however, their stories diverge. Leo, ruled by the Sun, is a royal sign, inheriting the crown by birthright. Capricorn, ruled by Saturn, the planet of mastery, is certainly the boss of the zodiac, earning that position through hard work. Both signs hope to leave a grand legacy for the future, but while Leo soaks in the attention of their fans, reveling in the spotlight, Capricorn sometimes feels lonely at the top. At least together they will have company, with Capricorn grounding Leo and Leo lighting up Capricorn's day.

There can be some awkward tension between them. Capricorn can seem so gloomy and rigid to Leo, who doesn't understand why Capricorn can't loosen up and party. Here's the thing: Capricorn can party. They've scheduled time for it in their planner. But Leo's go-to strategy of neutralizing discomfort by "having fun" doesn't fly with Capricorn. If Leo wants to get on the same page with Capricorn, they must achieve the maturity level beyond needing to have "fun" all the time; they need to be able to hold space for many feelings. In turn, Capricorn can show up for Leo by embracing the unconventional and making an effort to try new things and not be the curmudgeon on the block who yells at children not to skateboard on their lawn.

Leo gives themself fully in bed; they are totally passionate—something Capricorn really, deeply enjoys in a lover. Sex with Leo opens new doors of pleasure to Capricorn. And sex with Capricorn helps Leo ground into their body. If they live together, these two will need good security for all the expensive stuff they will purchase—they may have earned their fortune in different ways, but they have it nonetheless!

CAPRICORN & VIRGO

Productive is something both of these signs aspire to be in their daily lives, and together, not only do they offer each other support and a reliable sounding board, but they're able to have fun, too. They enjoy traveling and socializing. Many people don't realize that Capricorn loves to party, but Virgo sees this in them right away, offering them a drink, a dance, or a joke when they first meet. And Capricorn sees Virgo's intellect as hugely stimulating. They find Virgo cultured and well read, someone they can talk to about important things, whose opinion they value.

They must watch out for pessimism, though, as these two can complain to no end and be brutally negative. You don't want to know what this couple said about you after you left the party. If their text messages were published for the world to see, they would probably lose all their friends.

Fortunately, they're both fantastic at getting things done, so if they can find an important issue they're both passionate about, whether it's political, social, or personal, together they can make amazing changes happen.

In the bedroom, Capricorn is just who Virgo is looking for, and Capricorn enjoys the sexual adventures Virgo takes them on. Lots of lusty energy between these two—it's a hot one-night stand and a long-term relationship that stays interesting. Their home is warm and busy, work likely scattered everywhere.

Capricorn understands we don't have all the time in the world, while Virgo knows that practice and patience are key. Even though Capricorn says, "We don't have all day," and Virgo says, "It might take that long," somehow these two meet in the middle.

CAPRICORN & LIBRA

Capricorn was phony once at a business meeting, and it made them feel cheap and like a sellout, and they've never done it since. Being *real* is so important to Capricorn. Libra, on the other hand, is the diplomat, and that sometimes means putting on a nice, happy face. Is this being fake? Not to Libra. To Libra, this is kindness and fairness. Will Capricorn *get it*? Yes! Capricorn can be cool with Libra's different way of handling interactions, as long as Capricorn knows they are expressing their true emotions to them. Libra is able to hold space for them emotionally, as well, because Capricorn definitely won't pretend to like something they don't.

There's plenty of tension between these two, but lots to be gained as well: Capricorn is a hugely grounding energy for Libra, inspiring them to be firmer about their boundaries, and Capricorn

admires Libra's business sense and ability to partner with people. They can be a true power couple, not only making an impression in public, but also building a beautiful home together, exploring both fame *and* privacy.

It doesn't hurt that there is a lot of heat in the bedroom, too—Libra's dirty talk drives Capricorn wild, and Libra loves Capricorn's lusty and physical approach.

This is an exciting and dramatic one-night stand, and long term, these two will push each other to do incredible things. If they move in together, they'll enjoy a busy home—they just have to learn to trust each other and hammer out differences in communication. Libra shouldn't be afraid to be blunt, and Capricorn can help Libra out by taking the lead when Libra's dealing with decision fatigue.

CAPRICORN & SCORPIO

Capricorn and Scorpio are kindred spirits—both are enigmatic and lusty and share the same dry sense of humor. Scorpio is an intense sign, but Capricorn has never met anyone cooler, and Scorpio hasn't met anyone smarter than Capricorn! However, they will have to make an effort to consistently talk about their needs, instead of hiding them from each other. Communication is what makes and keeps this relationship strong.

Brilliant creativity flows between them, making a solid foundation for friendship and commitment, but these two dirty-minded individuals certainly can have some raunchy one-night stands, too. Together, they share a house filled with antiques and beautiful furniture. It's an enviable home—and envy is something they both know a lot about. They need to be careful about not letting it take over their relationship.

Being controlling is something they need to watch out for, too—they should save the power struggles for consensual fun in the bedroom, not in the car on the way to work, when they are at their peak of stress, anticipating what nonsense they'll have to deal with while they keep everything together for everyone.

When stress comes up, they need to remember what makes them best friends. They should visit a place together that reminds them of their past as well as what kind of future they *really* want to have. Capricorn, when they close their eyes, can hear life's clock ticking, and Scorpio knows that death greets us all. They must ask themself, "What do we want these precious moments to be filled with?"

CAPRICORN & SAGITTARIUS

Sagittarius is a great big mystery to Capricorn—this will either totally frustrate or totally excite them. Capricorn isn't into playing guessing games, and while Sagittarius is one of the most straight-shooting signs in the zodiac, some confusion between these two may still take place.

Once communication issues have been sorted, these two will have a wonderful time exploring spirituality and sharing secrets. Sagittarius learns a lot about responsibility through Capricorn, as well as issues concerning self-esteem. As attracted as they might be to one another, they still may feel some confusion about how to get along. Sagittarius would be wise to show their nurturing and protective side—a big, delicious meal can't hurt. And Capricorn should reveal their devilish streak that loves to party—but should also be sure to chat with their Sagittarius love frequently. They're both very direct people, and once the ice is broken, they can have lots of fun!

One thing they have in common, which they may not realize, is how focused they are on success: Capricorn dutifully climbs up the mountain, and Sagittarius aims their bow and arrow at the prize. The difference is that Sagittarius believes they'll make their mark, while Capricorn can feel uncertain about their upward ascent. They can learn a lot from each other—not to be more or less optimistic or pessimistic, but to celebrate when they reach their goals and to try again when they miss.

Their shared stamina in bed is sure to be exciting: Capricorn's presence is a fantastic match for Sagittarius's go-all-night attitude. Out of bed, these two need to be careful when they shop together. Capricorn is usually smart with money, but they can charge up a storm when they go shopping with Sagittarius. If they live together, their home will be their private sanctuary to escape from their public lives.

CAPRICORN & CAPRICORN

A total power couple, when two Capricorns come together, things get done. Oh, and they're hedonists, too. Enough has been said by astrologers about how this sign is a workaholic, so let's talk about the other things they take as seriously as making money: love and sex.

The energy in bed is hugely passionate—they're looking for someone who brings drama to the bedroom, and these two can totally supply that for each other. They're both kinky and open-minded, lusty and hugely physical. They both want to feel honored and worshiped by their lover, and they both crave loyalty from their partners.

Both are very goal oriented, and they'll need to be clear with each other about their intentions early on. This usually isn't a problem for straight-forward Capricorn; however, when you're working as hard and screwing as frequently as they do, it is actually possible to forget to have a conversation about such things. One thing people may not realize about Capricorn is that they can be quite forgetful—that's why they keep planners, notes, and Post-its everywhere. Yes, there are some very sharp Capricorns who don't forget a thing (and they'll remind you of your most embarrassing moments fifty years later), but generally, they need to write it down.

This pairing is quite intense as a fling . . . and intense in the long run, too! Their home is a lively one, with lots of shouting between the den and the bedroom about whose turn it is to cook. Sharing domestic duties will be something they need to sort out if they're going to live together.

CAPRICORN & AQUARIUS

Not much is a mystery to Aquarius, but they find Capricorn completely enigmatic, which keeps them totally intrigued—they're hooked! In Aquarius, Capricorn finds someone who is dependable and reliable, yet always coming up with novel, wacky ideas and happy to try new things. This relationship has both movement and stability. They share a planetary ruler, Saturn, the taskmaster of the zodiac, giving them a shared sense of responsibility.

Their shared snarky sense of humor brings them together, and their mutual respect for the other's independence and true friendship keeps them together. However, just a fling will be fun, too! They're both excitedly kinky in bed, their dressers filled to the brim with sex toys, lube, and sexy outfits. They get turned on in different ways, but that doesn't mean they can't give each other what they need: Capricorn should send some sexy texts during the day, and Aquarius should give Capricorn a deep massage to warm up.

Aloof Aquarius would also be wise to put their good listening skills to use—both have been accused by popular astrology of being cold and unfeeling. However, when Capricorn needs to vent and process, they really need their partner to be there. In turn, Capricorn should do their best to try to say at least one positive, jovial, lighthearted thing for every complaint, eye roll, or depressing rant they feel like sharing, for Aquarius's sake.

CAPRICORN & PISCES

These two will have plenty to discuss. For example, is time linear, like Capricorn's ascent up the mountain? Or is it cyclical, like Pisces's fish laps around the ocean? These two signs are very different in many ways—Capricorn is very literal; Pisces, more abstract—but these two can be the best of friends, as communication is one of their strong suits.

Capricorn admires Pisces's romantic nature and imagination, and Pisces thinks Capricorn is plain *cool*—they want to meet all their friends and hear all their ideas about the world. Their sex life is full of imagination: Pisces brings the wildest scenes, to Capricorn's delight.

If they live together, their home is sure to be a busy place, and while their approach to finances is very different, if these two go into business, the combination of Capricorn's industrious nature and Pisces's artistry is sure to be a success. "I like the way you think," Capricorn tells Pisces, to everyone's surprise. *Really?* they think. *That flaky fish? Capricorn is listening to what that dreamer has to say?* Of course, Capricorn knows that different perspectives can come together to create amazing ideas.

Pisces isn't sure if time exists. *I mean, it's man-made, isn't it?* they think. What's Capricorn to do with this information? They've been living with such certainty that the clock is ticking. Whatever the truth, in each other's embrace, time certainly doesn't exist.

AQUARIUS

WATER BEARER

DATES: JANUARY 20–FEBRUARY 19

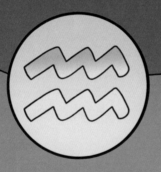

PLANETARY RULER: SATURN AND URANUS
ELEMENT: AIR
MODALITY: FIXED

PERSONALITY

A winter storm finds you snowed in. In this log cabin, there's no internet, no television, no radio, no telephone. What brilliance can be born from what most people would consider boredom? Welcome to Aquarius's mind.

The genius of the zodiac, this Air sign's mind never shuts down. A fixed sign, meaning their sign falls in the middle of a season—in this case, winter—Aquarius has focus and fortitude. A perennial scholar, Aquarius loves to study how things work, whether the subject is cutting-edge technology, home remedies with backyard herbs, or relationships and the people around them.

Unconventional, Aquarius creates their own path and stays true to who they are. They become fully immersed in whatever subjects or social scenes interest them. They're fantastic organizers and networkers. Ruled by Saturn, they're mature and serious, but ruled by Uranus, they crave freedom, making them reliable, yet unconventional, people.

AT THEIR BEST

Aquarius is a totally original, unique, visionary, progressive individual who values free thinking, innovation, and experimentation. These humanitarians are eager to raise the consciousness of those around them. Aquarius is a deep thinker, ambitious, and brilliantly inventive when they're able to focus their powerful mind. Revolution follows Aquarius wherever they go.

AT THEIR WORST

Aquarius overthinks things, getting stuck in their own heads and replaying scenarios, making them tense and exhausted. They can be stubborn when they are convinced of something: they don't want to feel like all that overthinking to get to where they are now has gone to waste! As cool and aloof as Aquarius may be, when they lose their temper, you can expect them to be cutting and mean. They know that words hurt, and they know which ones will slice you.

LOVE PERSONALITY

Behind the cold, cool exterior is someone who longs for a partner to explore and enjoy life with. Pop astrology sometimes calls our Aquarius friends robotic or alien, but this is a misunderstanding of their detached, scientific mind. Aquarius is very cerebral, but they're not all brains . . . they have a heart, too. So, what's the water bearer like in love? When they've found someone who awakens their passion, Aquarius is a present, thoughtful, and reliable partner, unmovable in their devotion—a best friend until the very end. Aquarius fears being stuck or trapped in a relationship that's based on social norms or expectations rather than real feelings; don't expect marriage plans after graduation followed by a baby with Aquarius just because that's "what everyone does." Aquarius doesn't do what everyone does, and when they love you, you know it's not out of obligation. It's for real.

FIRST IMPRESSIONS

It's easy to be intimidated by an Aquarius. Their fashion is very cool, they always seem to have the latest tech, plus they typically wear serious expressions. "You have resting bitch face" is certainly something they have heard once or twice, and they've been accused of being standoffish or cold. They can appear to be detached, but it's not out of cruelty. Their rational mind enables them to step back from a situation and observe things from a logical perspective, whether it is to see how things break down . . . or how they come together.

But they have their silly moods, too, and they have no qualms about showing them off to those close to them. If you meet them through friends, perhaps at a small dinner, they'll feel totally comfortable being their wacky selves, instead of the chill demeanor they usually wear for the world. Their sense of humor and seemingly breezy attitude could make you feel like you're instant best friends—but you're not. Aquarius needs space. And time. They want to get to know you, and they want you to get to know the real them, not just what their surface shows you.

If you meet them online, be creative and entertaining about how you contact them—a boring "Hi" isn't going to cut it. If you spot them at a party or concert, make sure they're giving you some eye contact before you approach them. They don't really like being approached unexpectedly. Sure, they're aloof, but they're just like anyone else—they'll check you out if they're interested!

FLIRTING TECHNIQUES

Aquarius is an Air sign, the element of communication, so if they like you, you will hear from them. Witty and a word-smith, they love banter, so keep it sharp and intellectual, and rely on them to share some exciting stories with you, too. They're not always the chattiest people, but when they have a crush, they usually have an interesting "You'll never believe *this*" tale to share. They enjoy hearing their phone regularly ping with a notification, and appreciate someone who is straightforward and regular with communication. Don't be afraid to make the first move—Aquarius is excited about people who are excited about them! Not sure what to talk about? Aquarius is attracted to the unusual and to mysteries, so ask them if they've seen the premiere of a sci-fi or detective show. As humanitarians, they're also into politics, so ask what they think about a news item—one you're genuinely passionate about. Knowing you care about the world is a turn-on for them.

Be a rebel. Aquarius loves rule breakers and people who aren't afraid to stand out in a crowd. Aquarius needs their space, so being clingy is bound to push them away. It's not that they're averse to hanging out all the time—they totally can—but if you make them feel like you can't live without them or that they're not free to do their own thing, they'll run the other way. Do not judge an Aquarius by their cover. Never jump to conclusions about situations or people just because of what's on the surface; Aquarius finds that very immature.

DATING STYLE

Prove you are reliable by keeping the dates you've planned, but also show you're not boring by being spontaneous; ruled by structure-oriented Saturn and rebel Uranus, Aquarius really needs *both* in their life: rules *and* breaking the rules.

Aquarius enjoys planning events, so they'll likely have an itinerary set up already if they call to ask you out. If you're planning the date, Aquarius loves going on adventures, so arrange an excursion: Visit a nearby neighborhood the two of you have never been to before, and swing by the most popular food joint—even better, surprise them with a random road trip to an unusual place, like the Whispering Gallery in Grand Central Station in New York City or the Wave Organ in San Francisco. Think of the strangest gallery, oddities store, restaurant, or monument, and take them there. They'll bring their camera (Aquarius usually has at least a few), and you two will have some lasting memories.

Go someplace where you can talk—a movie probably isn't the best first-date option, because they want to get to know you (and anyway, Aquarius is not the type to feel awkward going to a movie alone). They also don't mind spending a night in playing board games or watching movies—in fact, watching movies at home is great because they can talk over the actors as much as they like without getting kicked out of the theater.

When you're on the date, don't come across as a name-dropper or poseur, or judge people harshly for having different tastes than you. Nothing is less cool to an Aquarius than someone not being themself or not respecting other people's interests.

RELATIONSHIP APPROACH

Friendship is crucial to Aquarius, so nurture that aspect of your partnership as much as possible. Aquarius's cool demeanor can make it seem like they are unemotional, but that's totally untrue. They feel very deeply, but they value communicating their feelings in a thoughtful, organized, straightforward way.

Do not be surprised if you hear clinical-sounding terminology during an emotional conversation or argument with an Aquarius; they feel very comfortable using psychologist-approved lines as a way to express their feelings. One Aquarius told me that she had a book on effective communication for office managers—and that she pulled lines from it to use in her relationships.

Open-minded Aquarius approaches each relationship as a totally unique experience, not expecting past relationship formats to conform to the new. Their independence is also important to them, and they want a partner who has a life, too. Aquarius loves mysteries, but don't be one. Don't bother hiding things from them, as they are excellent detectives and will figure out the truth.

Take the initiative at work, at home, and in the relationship. Aquarius loves being around a go-getter who makes things happen, but they also need space—they need the perfect balance of a reliable best friend they can always count on, but without a clingy vibe. Be interested in life: Go places, meet people, learn things. Aquarius is attracted to people who are curious about the world. If you don't have a life, Aquarius won't want to be in yours.

SEX

"Predictable" is rarely a word used to describe Aquarius; however, in bed, you may find that your Aquarius lover has certain ol' reliable routines, kinks, toys, or techniques that regularly work for them. Don't mess with their process! Call them "boring" for their routines, and expect to be called judgmental and never hear from them again. Never kink-shame anyone—Aquarius in particular has been called weird too many times in their life to need to hear it from a partner.

Aquarius is totally up for experimenting and trying new things, too, and they'll be excited if you open up to them about what turns you on. Approach them directly; if you beat around the bush, it might confuse them. As an Air sign, Aquarius values verbal communication, from talking dirty to discussing boundaries.

Aquarians have a lot on their minds—declutter the space and make the bed nicely for them so they can forget about the world and focus on the moment. Get them going by having lots of dirty talk—Aquarius needs mental stimulation. Aquarius has a voyeuristic streak, so show them how hot they make you.

On a spiritual level, partner sex and masturbation are opportunities for Aquarius to merge their minds with their bodies.

TURN-ONS

Uranus, one of Aquarius's planetary rulers, governs electricity, so any high-tech sex toy is welcome in the bedroom. Porn is great, but Aquarius likes video chatting with real people as well, or being invited to a sex party. If you're with a shier

Aquarius, have them describe to you something they saw once that really turned them on, and then recreate it together. They are often voyeurs or exhibitionists (or both!).

Pick up some sexy uniforms to bring into the bedroom. Role-play doctor and patient, or cleaning person and home-owner. Play truth or dare—ask them about their most perverted fantasies, and then dare them to explore the possibility of trying it with you.

Innocence and purity are things Aquarius often gets off on, although the Uranian side of Aquarius is often attracted to rebels and weirdos. Submissive Aquarius enjoys taking orders or doing tasks. A dominant Aquarius will enjoy making a checklist of chores and requirements for their sub to accomplish, and being ruled by Saturn, can take on the daddy or parental role easily.

They're turned on by a partner who is versatile and flexible, so be sure to pleasure them with both your mouth *and* your hands! Don't leave any part of their body unpleased—be thorough!

TURN-OFFS

Immaturity is a big turn-off—badly timed gross fart jokes, squealing childishly (particularly if it's with disdain) over something you see at a sex toy shop, or not practicing safe sex are no-nos.

Aquarius is a great friend who is happy to listen when a pal or lover feels insecure about themself. But in the bedroom, be as confident as you can—if you continually apologize for the zit on your face while you two are warming up, things could cool down, as Aquarius will become more interested in getting you zit cream than anything else.

251

AQUARIUS & ARIES

Aquarius has seen Aries around town—they have mutual friends and spend time in the same scene. Aquarius admires Aries from afar, confused about why the ram hasn't given them a glance. Aquarius needs to learn that Aries pretty much is only aware of what's right in front of them . . . and, luckily for Aquarius, once Aries does notice them, they'll make a quick beeline to their new crush!

Aries is absolutely enamored by Aquarius, thinking they're the coolest person they've ever met (and they would have met them sooner if they had slowed down, maybe stayed someplace for longer than thirty minutes before getting bored and moving on to the next party). Aries is passionate and impulsive, and hugely inspired and calmed by Aquarius's logical, detached, and chill energy. They are especially impressed by how diplomatic Aquarius can be—as well as how they can eviscerate anyone in a debate.

Aquarius falls in love with the ram's quick, sharp mind, their straightforward and honest way of communicating, and their curiosity. Aries is the first sign on the zodiac wheel, and naturally, they love to be first at anything. In bed, they'll likely have many firsts together, as well as plenty of excitement with toys and role-play—these two are fun in bed!

As they become closer, Aries will realize Aquarius's need for peace and quiet in their home (despite how wild they both can be when they are partying), and Aquarius will learn how sensitive Aries truly is, despite the strong, brave front they often put on.

AQUARIUS & TAURUS

Glamour isn't a vibe Aquarius typically chases after, but after they see Taurus's home, their closet full of designer clothes, and their fully stocked fridge, they realize that glamour is fabulous and definitely something they want more of in their life. And Taurus's energy is just so comfortable! At least, until they both start being too stubborn about something, like how they feel about a mutual friend or whether or not a book is worth reading. Aquarius enjoys debating things like this, but Taurus gets annoyed, or bored, or tired, and decides to take a nap, watch TV, or otherwise relax while Aquarius whips themself into a fury about how Taurus won't listen to them.

But that doesn't mean the sex won't be hot. Taurus's slow pace is absolutely thrilling to Aquarius, and their ability to be physically present takes their breath away. Meanwhile, Taurus is turned on by Aquarius's

imagination. Even though they might bicker, there is a lot these two can learn from each other. Taurus admires Aquarius's ability to be innovative—this is a quality they eagerly want to cultivate in themself.

Like Aquarius, Taurus has a reputation for being chill, but Taurus needs to know that if they play it *too* cool, it can be confusing to Aquarius, who is usually drawn to more over-the-top personalities. The same can be said for Taurus, who typically tends toward intense personalities—Aquarius's aloofness could be either refreshing or frustrating.

They should be clear about their needs and desires, and they ought to pick their battles. This is usually an exciting fling, as there is plenty of tension between them, but it can also work long term if they both have a sense of humor.

AQUARIUS & GEMINI

When Aquarius meets Gemini, their sketchbooks are suddenly full with doodles of their crush, poems they have inspired, and to-do lists for the dates they want to go on. These two Air signs have plenty of fun, as Aquarius thinks Gemini is one of the most exciting people they have ever met. Gemini is turned on by deep thinkers, so it is easy for them to fall for Aquarius.

They are both big communicators, and with all the texting that will take place between these two, they would be wise to carry around an extra charger with them. It's important that Aquarius tries to be romantic—sometimes Gemini thinks Aquarius is too cool for flowers and love letters, but they actually love it, and they can solidify a place in Gemini's heart by being romantic.

Gemini would be wise to display their fantastic people skills, as well as the side of them that is a creator or performer—and they need to be reliable. Yes, Aquarius has more fun with Gemini than anyone (which is why this is such a great fling), but if they're interested in something long term, Gemini needs to show that they're cool under pressure and can control their nerves. Aquarius also needs to show Gemini their adventurous spirit, which shouldn't be too hard, as well as be honest, which can sometimes be a little harder. This isn't to say that Aquarius is a liar, but they need to be open with Gemini; little secrets here and there won't work.

They have an exciting, electric sex life, filled with plenty of toys, porn subscriptions, and other partners they can bring in on the fun. If they choose to live together, they need to have space for work (Gemini often takes theirs home) and for play (Aquarius needs a place to lounge).

AQUARIUS & CANCER

Aquarius probably first saw Cancer at the local coffee shop—some mornings, Cancer would be in a fun, light mood; other days, they were all business; and sometimes...they did not show up at all. When that break in routine happens, Aquarius is surely sad to miss out on enjoying the company of their crab crush.

When things elevate from crush to friend, Aquarius finds that during the time they spend with Cancer they learn how to maintain supportive routines and rituals that help them stay organized and healthy—Cancer is a nurturer, and their habits often rub off on others. Kicking bad habits will be a theme for them both, and they will learn to move on from the past as they spend time together—especially the crab, who sometimes clings to the past too tightly.

Cancer has a reputation for being very emotional, while Aquarius does not. While you might think this would make them incompatible (and it's true they will have to make a lot of adjustments for this relationship to work), their temperamental differences can absolutely create an exciting energy between them. Cancer helps Aquarius connect with their emotions, and Aquarius inspires Cancer to detach from their nostalgic tendencies and look at things more logically.

In bed, they will discover that the cautious crab is way more uninhibited than they seem—likely less so than Aquarius! Aquarius is known for being the inventor of the zodiac, and Cancer is always up for trying something new, making this an unexpectedly electrifying combination. Even if it's just a short fling, an awkward moment or two is likely. Cancer's moods typically don't bother Aquarius, who also needs to have space in relationships, as long as Cancer is good about communicating what's going on.

AQUARIUS & LEO

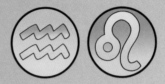

Cool Aquarius running into warm Leo can be a perfect match—or a perfect disaster. Leo is Aquarius's opposite sign on the zodiac wheel. As such, a partnership brings them unique perspectives about themselves and their needs, boundaries, and desires. Aquarius's chill vibe contrasts with Leo's sunny disposition. Opposites attract, but these two can certainly create drama as well.

They are both stubborn—Leo wants what they want, and to Aquarius, there is no arguing with logic—but in a strange way, they admire this about each other. They both appreciate someone who sticks to their vision (as long as the vision isn't small-minded).

In the bedroom, it would be wise to bring in Leo's element, Fire, to help set the mood—Leo loves drama, so Aquarius should deck the space with candlelight or get an impressive fire going in a firepit outside, where they can make out under the stars (Leo loves getting affectionate in nature). In turn, Leo should be sure to talk to Aquarius about what turns them on.

Living together is surely one of the most intense things these two will do in their relationship, and balancing private/personal life is an important part of their success as a couple. They need clear communication about what they want shared with the world and what is private—before Leo starts posting selfies in bed, with Aquarius sleeping next to them, on social media.

AQUARIUS & VIRGO

Aquarius wants to see great change take place in the world; however, when they date a Virgo, the question they must ask is, how ready are they to undergo transformation of their own? Spending time with Virgo helps them face their vulnerabilities, and they are going to have to let go of the past if they want to move toward a future with them.

These two will find themselves in a constant state of rebirth when they spend time together, whether they just have a one-night stand or spend the rest of their lives together. Learning to share—both emotionally and materially—is also a major lesson for Aquarius during their time with Virgo.

As Virgo spends time with Aquarius, they too will have to make transformations, as they will be pushed to let go of bad habits and develop healthier self-care routines. Their mutual love of structure and logic is fantastic; however, Aquarius will need to show their weird and whimsical side if they want to win Virgo over romantically. They are both highly introspective people, but their communication styles are different—as are their arguing styles.

In bed, the energy is sensual yet often carnal. If it's a one-night stand, it will either be the most awkward or most amazing of their lives. If they stay together, their home will be warmly decorated, with a fully stocked fridge that Virgo will likely need to edit if there is too much junk.

AQUARIUS & LIBRA

Libra likely caught Aquarius's eye in some situation where they were able to notice how cultured and intelligent Libra is. They have plenty in common, from their intellectual interests to how they like to have fun. Libra is a sign that loves to party and socialize—they can get along with anyone, but there is a kind of humor they share with Aquarius that they can't get with most people.

While they certainly have a good time and easy conversation, if they want something lasting, Aquarius will have to show Libra that they are eager to continue working on themself and conquer their goals. Libra is a go-getter, but also a people pleaser—they will resent Aquarius if they drag them down into a complacent routine.

One Libra, while talking about her Aquarius ex, said to me, "God, do you know how many times I saw him in sweatpants?!" Don't be that Aquarius, dear Aquarius reader. Additionally, if Aquarius wants to make their Libra partner happy, give them compliments. Libra hears that they're smart from everyone, but it's from their partner that they get the juicier compliments.

Libra has a reputation for being one of the sweetest, most popular signs in the zodiac, but Aquarius should be careful: they can have just as sharp a tongue as the water bearer. A fight between them is a terrible electrical storm . . . but for the most part, these two Air signs are willing to talk and compromise.

AQUARIUS & SCORPIO

Aquarius reminds Scorpio of someone they once knew, maybe in a past life. Scorpio is emotionally intense, so being around Aquarius's cool, sharp, logical mind is a comforting thing for them. Aquarius's ability to make sense of the things (and feelings) that confound them is one of the reasons Scorpio values them so much.

Plus, they're both into strange and unusual things, like paranormal phenomena and true crime stories. They can stay up all night talking about mysteries, politics, and their mutual favorite topic: people's motivations.

Scorpio's ambition is highly inspiring to Aquarius, especially on a professional level. If Aquarius was slacking on their goals before they met Scorpio, they will be especially eager to get their shit together once they spend some time with the scorpion.

Scorpio wants them to share their deepest secrets, so Aquarius would be wise to arrive on a date with some personal and intriguing story to share. There's plenty of tension to keep the spark in bed going for a long time. Living together isn't something they should jump into without thorough consideration, but if everything is planned well, and they're open to compromise, it can totally work.

When Aquarius gets stressed out, they ruminate on how to solve the problem. When Scorpio gets stressed out, their world ends. They don't think about fixing it—they throw it in the trash and, if possible, light it on fire (they're pretty dramatic once you get to know the mysterious scorpion, FYI), and are reborn like the phoenix. Will this inspire or frustrate Aquarius? Only time will tell.

AQUARIUS & SAGITTARIUS

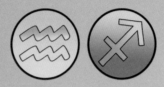

Aquarius is a freethinking rebel, but that does not mean they are free from gloom, unlike Sagittarius, who more often than not sees the glass half full—a quality of theirs that rubs off nicely on Aquarius. Aquarius rubs off on them nicely, too: despite how well read and eager for new experiences Sag is, they can also be stuck on a high horse sometimes, and Aquarius is more than happy to knock them off.

These two are sure to have plenty of fun with each other—Sagittarius always says what is on their mind, and their blunt way of communicating is hilarious to Aquarius, who easily falls in love with and admires Sag's sharp, inventive mind. The banter between them flows easily, which is truly the ticket to Aquarius's heart.

These two are sure to share a busy social calendar as well as do plenty of travel—surprising Sagittarius with a trip is never a bad idea for Aquarius. In bed, Sagittarius is vocal about their desires, which is a huge turn-on for the water bearer, who can ignite Sagittarius's passion by surprising them with unexpected romance—especially the kind they can physically indulge in, like fancy wines or chocolates. There isn't a Sagittarius who doesn't dream of hours of sex interspersed with breaks to sip champagne and nibble a macaron, while wearing a silk robe in a big, fluffy, cozy bed.

Long term, if they choose to live together, Aquarius will need to make space for Sagittarius's altars, while Sag will need to be better about splitting the fridge. These two make solid friends (or friends with benefits!).

AQUARIUS & CAPRICORN

Aquarius can solve pretty much any puzzle—except Capricorn, who absolutely confounds them. Aquarius finds the sea goat baffling, and therefore irresistible—even more than a good mystery. Spending time with Capricorn will have them facing emotions they had been avoiding or did not realize were there.

Aquarius teaches Capricorn things, too: Capricorn discovers much about their sense of self-worth through their relationship with the water bearer. Capricorn is industrious and a hard worker, but they secretly sometimes wonder if they're innovative enough; Aquarius is the perfect partner to help them shake things up.

They are both ruled by Saturn, a cold and somber planet, so when things heat up between them, the energy that results from their warmth is truly unique. They have a rare, special kind of connection. These two signs have an understanding about the limited time we have here on Earth to make a difference, to connect, and to love one another, something that not every other sign understands as intimately as they do.

If they live together, it will hopefully be a spacious place, because they both need their own areas to think and work (something they respect tremendously about each other), as well as a comfortable room for them to share a smoke, a drink, and a laugh (they share the same sense of gallows humor).

AQUARIUS & AQUARIUS

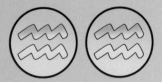

People have asked me if dating your own sign feels like dating yourself. Not really, and especially not so for Aquarius, because this sign is all about being unique and unlike anyone else. Every Aquarius is their own personal brand of water bearer.

That said, they of course have things in common, like needing to be with a partner who is capable of discussing anything from the most emotional to the most mundane matter with tact, clarity, and timeliness. They crave a warm home to retreat to when they need space from the world they are so deeply trying to change for the better, and a partner who is grounded, secure, and confident.

Communication is hugely important to them both, but breaking the ice initially could be a little intimidating—they should have a sense of humor, and be warm and direct when they do. Once they are acquainted, they will figure out how they feel about each other quickly . . . but they will likely still take time to develop a friendship first.

They shouldn't be shy to show off to each other, or to behave boldly, perhaps sending a video of themself serenading their partner with a love song. Will it embarrass them a little bit? Yes, but they both have a good sense of humor, and these grand gestures of romance are needed, or else these two water bearers might attempt to out-aloof each other.

The sexual energy between them is sure to be electric; however, if they really want their bodies to buzz with excitement, it is key that Aquarius brings practices into the bedroom that help them really get into their bodies, like spending time massaging or cuddling. If they move in together, their space is sure to be filled with both of their wacky collections and belongings.

AQUARIUS & PISCES

Aquarius is a genius, an idea machine. But when partnered with a Pisces they can bounce ideas off of, their brilliance gains an extra bit of magic, which is something that sometimes, on a sad day, Aquarius fears they're missing. They know they're smart, cool, and capable, but then Aquarius meets Pisces, this free spirit who makes amazing art, has psychic dreams, and can connect with anyone, and Aquarius wonders if they are a little too uptight, or gloomy, or detached, or, worse, not as creatively talented.

Here's the scoop, Aquarius: Pisces might not be uptight, but they have their own issues. They can also certainly be very gloomy—as the last sign in the zodiac, they've seen some shit. And creative talent? Well, Aquarius must know they're the genius of the zodiac, and that creativity is something *all* people can tap into. Perhaps it would make them feel better to know that Pisces finds them to be a total and complete mystery, which, being that they are psychic, is really quite a compliment!

These two will enjoy plenty of hours watching horror and sci-fi movies, talking about metaphysics and aliens, and exploring unusual places and ideas together. They are both individuals who value being unique.

Pisces is looking for a partner who is grounded and self-reflective, so Aquarius should show this side of themself. Pisces enjoys learning about psychology, but take note: if Aquarius uses clinical-sounding language during an argument, or overly intellectualizes their emotions, Pisces will get frustrated.

PISCES

THE FISH

DATES: FEBRUARY 19–MARCH 20

PLANETARY RULER: JUPITER AND NEPTUNE
ELEMENT: WATER
MODALITY: MUTABLE

PERSONALITY

A siren's song lures you to a dangerous edge . . . should you take the leap? Is this the end, or the beginning of something new?

Pisces is the last sign of the zodiac, and as such, feels like an old soul to many of us and to themself, too. Ruled by Jupiter, the planet of expansion, and Neptune, a dreamy and imaginative planet named for the god of the sea, Water sign Pisces is deep and emotional. The last sign of the winter season, Pisces is an empathetic, flexible, changeable, mutable sign.

Although they are dreamers, they also want to *do* something on this planet. Ruled by beneficent Jupiter, Pisces often wants "to leave the world a better place" than the way it was when they were born.

AT THEIR BEST

Pisces people are creatives. They think symbolically and will totally get it when you say something abstract, like, "I'm feeling pink today." They are empathic and go above and beyond for the people they care about. They sincerely love making people happy—and they're not afraid to sit with people who are in pain, sad, or going through a hard time. They are highly intuitive. They know what the next big trends are just as well as they know what outfit you're likely to wear that evening.

AT THEIR WORST

The moody, evasive Pisces can be deceptive, changeable, and confused. These escape artists flake on plans, and often react with extreme sensitivity to any question or challenge. These spacey martyrs can be weak willed, insecure, self-pitying, and unreliable. The truth is subjective, and in fact, they can see the truth in multiple sides of any story, which at times may make people accuse them of being two-faced.

LOVE PERSONALITY

Fantastical and whimsical, Pisces wants to be swept off their feet. Yes, they're fish, which means they have fins, but romantic Pisces is a poet who doesn't mind a metaphor. But there is a secret side to Pisces, as well. They need to hide sometimes. They enjoy being alone, in the dark, especially by the ocean, where they can listen to the waves and process their many emotions—both happy and sad. Recharging is important to Pisces—and so is love. They really believe in it, and when they find it, they cherish it.

Pisces seeks growth, understanding, and unity—love is part of how they achieve this. But finding happiness can be hard for Pisces. Being told they are too imaginative and sensitive can make them second-guess themself and reality.

It's also easy for them to get wrapped up in someone else's ideas about love: Pisces can become anything for anyone, but that doesn't mean that's what's good for them. The faster they learn this lesson, the sooner they'll find fulfillment in relationships with people who appreciate who they are instead of morphing into a weird version of themself for someone else. Pisces gives and gives, sometimes feeling uncomfortable taking, asking for help, or saying no. Boundaries are an important lesson for Pisces to learn, and when they do, their relationships transform into much healthier, happier ones.

FIRST IMPRESSIONS

When you meet a Pisces, you'll notice that they talk out their thought process, especially if they're busy, feel nervous, or think you're cute. Because these fish frequently overbook themselves, get flustered, and love to love, it's likely that all three scenarios are the case. They can be clumsy, as this cosmic Water sign can lose track of where they end and you—or the table, or the corner of the wall they're about to stub their toe on—begin. But they can also be graceful.

They often love dance, art, and music. They may be carrying a strange book when you first meet—aliens, astrology, unsolved mysteries, or detective stories: if it's weird or whimsical, they'll like it. They might smell like patchouli, but you'll get used to it, just like you'll get used to their love of loud and eccentric fashion.

These visionary people, who sometimes get lost in their heads, are craving union, ecstasy, enlightenment, and connection with something bigger, greater, beyond us. If they're overwhelmed by their surroundings, they find themself "checking out"—propagating their flaky or dreamy reputation—in order to preserve their energy. Encounter Pisces in a physically—and psychically—comfortable location, and you'll be struck by their intuitive abilities and what a great listener they are.

FLIRTING TECHNIQUES

Pisces doesn't have the biggest ego, but like any of us, they love compliments, so break the ice with a personal compliment to get the conversation going. If you two meet online, be sure to have a variety of photos for Pisces to peruse—this sign loves photography and hates a limited selection of anything.

If they catch your eye in person, see if you can get a mutual friend to introduce you—as friendly and flirty as Pisces might be, it can be draining for them to be approached by a stranger unexpectedly. As you're building rapport, be clear that you're romantically interested, because the "do they like me/don't they like me" noise will be stressful for them if it's not clarified quickly. And don't bet that they're always going to be clear about asking you if you're interested, because these fish can be shy, and they don't like to be embarrassed.

Do share some of your vulnerabilities—they want depth. Flirtation that's too light and airy won't make the impact you need. Dreamy Pisces might seem ditzy, but don't be fooled—they crave intellectual connection. Having something smart to say about a movie you recently saw or a book you just read is a huge turn-on.

DATING STYLE

If they ask you out (which, if they do, congrats, because these fish are bashful), they'll likely suggest something that involves music, art, nature, or an activity that takes you two out of mundane, everyday life.

Take them to get food someplace that only locals know about—they love being insiders, but don't necessarily care about the pomp that comes with being VIPs. Have them garden or walk your dog with you—they'll be touched, not annoyed, that you want to include them in your daily routine.

Being organized and having a schedule helps keep Pisces feeling safe and contained—they adore people who have it "together" in this regard; however, spontaneity comes naturally to them, so expect to be asked out on some random dates!

RELATIONSHIP APPROACH

The sometimes flaky Pisces knows there are many fish in the sea. If they're not interested in committing, you probably won't have to wonder for very long, because they'll be out of your line of sight before you can ask, "What are we?"

But not all fish flake, and many are totally comfortable in commitments, especially if you two are able to process your emotions together productively. Whether you're in a monogamous or polyamorous relationship, if you are kind and open about your needs you'll rarely see them jealous or possessive, although they can be paranoid. In polyamorous relationships, it's important that all parties discuss how much they want to disclose for there to be open and ongoing con-versations about boundaries.

Allow them to be open with their needs, too, and don't judge them—if you do, issues like paranoia about what you're up to behind their back may come up, or they might get up to something behind *your* back. If you want to settle down, don't frighten your Pisces by alluding to the idea that you plan on doing an over-the-top marriage proposal in public, with song and dance. PDA is a no-no, especially if it's too mushy; the attention it will draw to them is a lot for them to handle!

If you argue with your Pisces lover, avoid using clinical jargon that sounds like something you pulled from a book about effective communication—this is sure to piss them off. They want to talk about feelings, but are very annoyed by emotions being theorized or talked about in a contrived way. They want to know they're fighting with you, not the author of a self-help book (which, honestly, is one of their guilty pleasure favorite genres!).

Also, don't be unnecessarily negative. They already know life can suck. They are well acquainted with the feeling that "I didn't ask to be born!" The world's pain weighs on them heavily. Whining about how stupid a friend's outfit is and being pettily negative is a turn-off.

SEX

Pisces's artistry extends into the bedroom, where they enjoy living out their many fantasies: They are up for just about anything, even though they can be protective about discussing their needs in bed until they really trust someone. Ask them what their fantasies are—this dreamy sign is sure to have a few!

They are romantic, passionate lovers who often tap into their profound intuitive abilities while making love. Go slow with Pisces in the bedroom—being rushed is a turn-off for them; however, that doesn't mean they are totally averse to quickies, especially if it's to say "goodbye" before you two head out.

Don't be surprised if they stare deeply into your eyes, as if they're expressing something to you psychically. Do your best to open up and receive the message! Tell them they're the sexiest person you've ever met. Be romantic and sexy, but not sappy. Yes, Pisces is a total sap, but keep it out of the bedroom—they want to hear you speak to them in a sexy tone of voice, not a mushy one, while in bed!

Pisces tends to walk in danger's way, but they really need safety in bed, so romance them by creating as comfortable a space as possible. Light an incense you know they love, dim the lights to a comfortable glow, and make sure there will not be any distractions or disruptions, like buzzing cell phones or screaming neighbors.

Through sex with a partner or masturbation, Pisces achieves the sort of unity that their spirit longs for. Life is messy for these fish—and connecting sexually helps them achieve a feeling of balance; things just *make sense* after Pisces orgasms.

TURN-ONS

Pisces is generous, both in bed and out, and while they probably won't remember what you spent on their birthday gift, they *will* remember if you were stingy in bed.

Pisces rules the feet, and while I could suggest you massage them, kissing them reverently is even better: Pisces wants to be worshiped! Pisces may be passive in everyday life; however, in the bedroom they can be unexpectedly dominant, enjoying taking control, teasing their lovers and making them beg for more.

Whether dominant or submissive, Pisces enjoys the fantasy aspect of sex, and wearing costumes or setting imaginative scenes turns them on. A submissive Pisces often enjoys doing tasks for their partner, or simply surrendering to their every wish.

Feed them dessert slowly, and then have sex on the dinner table. Pisces needs variety as much as they crave safety in bed. Speaking of safety, let them know you will protect them—hold them close, and let them know that you can be counted on.

TURN-OFFS

Being any kind of fake or phony is a huge turn-off for Pisces. Never tell them you worship the ground they walk on if you don't.

Safety and privacy are important for Pisces to feel like they can open up in bed. Don't suggest live-streaming your romp unless you two have already established that you're both into it!

Never kink-shame anyone, but especially not Pisces; if they expose themself so vulnerably to you, it means they really trust you. Let them know what your limits are early on if you're worried you might unknowingly kink-shame them, so they'll know, for example, not to let you in on their furry fantasy.

PISCES & ARIES

There is a strong and unusual bond between these two: They both occupy unique spots on the zodiac wheel, with Aries as the first sign and Pisces as the last. The beginning and the end: what profound spaces to occupy.

Being in the presence of Aries makes Pisces feel like everything is going to be okay. After spending time with their Aries friend, Pisces will leave feeling like they've just listened to the most uplifting pep talk of their lives—usually. Being around the ram brings Pisces's self-esteem issues to the forefront, which can either be deeply healing or can stir up some insecurities. But this is not one-sided! Pisces's mysterious, sometimes hard to read, dreamy demeanor also stirs self-doubt in the ram . . . but this same enigmatic quality is what draws Aries in!

Aries also deeply admires how considerate Pisces is of others as well as their ability to connect with all kinds of people, so Pisces should not play down these aspects of their personality. Aries should show how productive they can be (Pisces is wowed by this)—and patient, too, which isn't easy for Aries but is something they can achieve with practice.

This combination of signs is an intense fling. In the bedroom, the energy is deeply emotional. If this becomes long term, they'll have to talk about how to do things at home, as Pisces may have random friends crash on the couch, and Aries is much more uptight about who they let into their personal space.

PISCES & TAURUS

As the last sign in the zodiac, Pisces doesn't have the biggest ego; therefore, it may come as a surprise to them just how *cool* Taurus thinks they are. Pisces's imagination, style, friends, and dreams all inspire Taurus. And the feeling is mutual—Pisces thinks Taurus is pretty cool, too. Pisces admires Taurus's ability to be present in the moment (something that can be difficult for the daydreaming Pisces), their knowledge of all the delicious food spots, and their baskets full of beauty and bath products—Pisces loves digging through Taurus's loot. Pisces is not usually materialistic, but when they're wearing Taurus's plush robe the morning after, they realize that they could really get used to that lifestyle!

A friendship between Pisces and Taurus develops easily, and it's the effortlessness that's felt between the two that's especially touching to Taurus. Taurus is famous for being stubborn, and Pisces is sure to notice that Taurus is not as flexible when it comes to decision making as they are; however, Pisces's easygoing attitude can be a good influence on Taurus. Taurus's grounding energy is psychically calming to Pisces, and Taurus pushes the fish to get clear on things they might otherwise weigh endlessly. To seduce Taurus, Pisces needs to be sure to keep them well fed, and to lend them their coziest sweater when it gets cold.

Pisces's intuition combined with Taurus's sensuality makes for a phenomenal time in the bedroom. This union is fine as a fling (they can be fantastic friends with benefits!) and works easily long term because these two are best friends, sharing a lively and exciting home.

PISCES & GEMINI

Gemini isn't the only pair of twins in the zodiac; Pisces is symbolized by two fish. While on the surface, Pisces and logical Air sign Gemini may not have much in common, this combination is surely one of the most exciting when falling in love. Pisces feels at home with Gemini: their talkative, cheerful, and curious nature allows Pisces to feel comfortable around them, and Pisces's creativity is hugely inspiring to Gemini, influencing them to push things further in their own careers.

Plenty of conversation is to be had between the fish and the twins; however, communication issues may flare up when Pisces finds that Gemini takes things very literally (Pisces has a more generous relationship with language!). Water sign Pisces would also be wise not to take it too personally if Gemini needs more time to communicate their feelings than they're used to: it's critical to Gemini to use the right words when expressing their love for someone, while Pisces thinks it's just fine to whip up an abstract collage proclaiming their affection.

When trying to seduce Gemini, Pisces must remember to be confident and believe in themself. They need to speak about themself in a way that they would want others to talk about them. Being casually self-deprecating may lead Gemini to think Pisces doesn't *want* them to like them, or that they live in a word of anxious delusions, instead of in the reality logical Gemini is always trying to make sense of. And playful Gemini appears to be easygoing about everything; however, Pisces may find that they're picky and detail oriented. Their home is sure to be filled with media—books, albums, and playlists, with movies waiting to be watched. These two will always have plenty to talk about!

PISCES & CANCER

Cancer has a reputation for being the nurturing homemaker; however, this is not the side that Pisces first notices when the crab catches their eye. Pisces sees someone who is endlessly entertaining—a show they never want to stop watching!—a person who inspires them creatively, makes them laugh, and takes them to fantastic parties. Cancer is also excited about Pisces, who can help the crab break out of their usual routines and explore unfamiliar places and new ideas.

The chemistry between these two signs is easy, but easy isn't always long lasting. Cancer is certainly a great choice for a quick fling for Pisces, but if Pisces is looking for a deeper commitment with the crab, it's crucial to show their ambitious and responsible side. Romance is also very important to Cancer, so Pisces should be sure to clean up and light some candles, and buy some chocolates and flowers. In turn, Cancer needs to display how reliable they can be—no disappearing acts into their shell for too long a time!

Cancer very intuitively understands what Pisces needs in bed—safety—and is very able to provide it. Cancer's ability to make loved ones feel protected is profound. And Pisces, always an enigma, has the mystery to keep Cancer aching for more time for closeness and connection.

If they live together, homemaker Cancer is sure to create an exciting place for Pisces to come home to. Whether this pair ends up as lovers or just friends, they should make art together—Pisces's imagination coupled with Cancer's talent for manifesting ideas into reality can lead to wonderful creations.

PISCES & LEO

If anyone could inspire Pisces to hit the salon, the gym, or the dental hygienist, it is Leo. Pisces sees Leo coming, and they quickly stomp out their cigarette. Pisces can sometimes have the reputation of a starving artist; however, when they develop a crush on Leo, suddenly they have a 9-to-5 to wake up for . . . they're not going to let Leo see them slacking!

But Leo ends up doing something quite different around Pisces—showing the side of themselves that's a "mess," even though this proud lion usually seems to "have it all" to everyone else. Pisces is comfortable with vulnerability, and being in their presence allows Leo to tap into their sensitive side—usually.

Sometimes the process of opening up and exploring pain is too difficult, so the lion may shy away. Pisces's psychic abilities freak out the lion from time to time. If, however, the lion is emotionally ready to enter the depths the fish is capable of exploring, this relationship will find both signs making major transformations in their lives. For Pisces, this means developing healthier habits, and for Leo, learning to let go of past pain as well as learning to share, both on a practical and an emotional level.

To seduce Leo, Pisces should show how unique they are. Leo needs to reveal how loyal and reliable they can be. These two can run into awkward moments as they get to know each other, and flings often happen unexpectedly, which excites them both!

Leo's love of drama mixed with Pisces's imagination makes for a good time in bed. If they stick together, Leo will find a way to decorate that will make Pisces's giant album collection more than just a pile of boxes they hadn't been able to sort through since the last time they moved. They have a lot to learn from each other!

PISCES & VIRGO

Virgo is Pisces's opposite sign, and being with Virgo helps Pisces gain new perspective about themself, love, and the world. Pisces is a dreamer; Virgo is a planner. Pisces thinks big; Virgo considers the details. Pisces wishes and dances in the moonlight; Virgo dutifully tends to a garden under the clear light of day. On the surface, Virgo may not seem as mystical as Pisces, the psychedelic fish, but this is very far from the truth: Virgos are deep thinkers, profoundly concerned with finding inner truth, which is something these two very much have in common.

They both also care deeply about helping others and healing the planet. The world often doesn't make sense, but things are crystal clear to Pisces when they are with Virgo. When Pisces wants to seduce Virgo, it shouldn't be too hard: despite what Virgo's name suggests, this Earth sign is quite lusty and will be up for whatever Pisces

has planned in the bedroom! They're both very giving partners, too. Virgo does very well when they have a checklist to work off of, so Pisces shouldn't be afraid to clearly state their needs, in bed and out.

Trust is very important to them both, if they're going to stay together in the long term. Virgo needs to try not to be so critical of sensitive Pisces, or else the fish may swim away, leaving Virgo worried—they can get into a bad cycle of this, if they don't watch out! Transparency is very important to Virgo, while Pisces can find Virgo's need to know what they're up to all day (and night) controlling—so again, trust is so important. Living in the right neighborhood is important to them if they choose to move in together, and if they don't and just keep it casual, being each other's local neighborhood friend with benefits works, too!

PISCES & LIBRA

Both Pisces and Libra have been picked on for being indecisive—Libra weighing what is the right thing to do, and Pisces seeing all sides to every situation. However, when it comes to each other, these two signs usually have a pretty quick grasp of the situation. Many find Pisces a mystery, but Libra sees the fish as clear as day. Some find Libra to be a superficial flirt, but Pisces is able to connect to a much deeper, emotional side of them, a side that's sensitive, spiritual, and complicated.

Whether it's a fling or something serious, these two will need to make plenty of adjustments to make things work—which could actually be okay, because they're both so accommodating! However, it's important that both maintain individual boundaries so they don't accommodate themselves into oblivion for each other.

There's a side to Pisces that's an adventurer, an optimist (despite all the difficulties they have seen), and eager to learn and grow. This is the side of Pisces that Libra is especially inspired by, so they would be wise to show it off! Libra should display how thoughtful, patient, and logical they can be—dreamy Pisces loves a down-to-earth person who *gets* and appreciates their fantastic imagination!

The energy in bed is romantic—lingerie, champagne, long conversations after multiple orgasms . . . unless Pisces falls asleep—if they stay up, they'll have so many profound things to say, but sometimes a cozy bed and a lover's arms are too relaxing to keep Pisces awake! That's fine—Libra will likely have someone else on speed dial to text if Pisces falls asleep! This can be an awkward or exciting fling, depending on whether or not Pisces and Libra are on the same page about who should take the lead, but long term, once these two get into the groove of things, they can build an exciting future, with a busy home.

PISCES & SCORPIO

Spending time with Scorpio will open doors for Pisces to see the world and enjoy new experiences. Although both can spend hours talking about philosophy and enjoying mind-expanding activities, and Scorpio doesn't have more fun with anyone than with Pisces, there are some key personality differences between them: Scorpio is much more defensive and decisive than Pisces. They can be frustrated by Pisces's seemingly flip-flop personality. But Pisces doesn't actually flip-flop. It just seems that way to the scorpion, a sign that comes prepared with a stinger. Scorpio has to learn that Pisces needs time to process the multitude of information their psyche sorts through before they choose a course of action—or in some cases, two courses. (*Why should anyone be limited?* thinks Pisces.) Scorpio is also perplexed by the fact that easygoing Pisces never seems jealous. Pisces does get jealous, but they believe we're all one—so why be jealous of yourself?

There's an instant feeling of comfort between these two Water signs; however, they should take things slowly. Trust is crucial, and jealousy or paranoia may screw things up. Pisces learned a long time ago that "letting go" is often the best option. Scorpio hasn't. Scorpio clings to power (sometimes overpowering Pisces!), and "letting go" is difficult for them to do.

In the bedroom, things are especially intense, as these two are eager to connect on a deep and emotional level that not everyone is prepared to experience. What does Scorpio have to learn from Pisces? How to let go, unwind, relax, celebrate, have fun, enjoy life, and take the massive amount of creative energy they have and make something with it. Pisces brings creative inspiration into Scorpio's life, and in return, they teach Pisces new ways of seeing the world. If they stick together, these two intense signs will need to make sure their home is a space where they can find peace, not drama!

PISCES & SAGITTARIUS

The tension between Pisces and Sagittarius is strong, making for a hugely passionate relationship! Both Pisces and Sagittarius are ruled by Jupiter, the benevolent planet of growth and good luck. Jupiter's expansive energy is expressed in Sagittarius as a desire to travel, study, and teach, and it is expressed in Pisces as a drive to explore and expand consciousness: These two both strive for enlightenment. They push each other to be bigger, better, and stronger than they were when they first met.

Pisces feels like home to Sagittarius, with their empathetic and artistic sensibilities, and Pisces finds Sagittarius easy to connect with spiritually. Sagittarius inspires Pisces to chase their dream on a professional level and to stand in the spotlight (which, oftentimes, Pisces is pretty shy about!).

The most important thing these two signs have in common is their belief that anything is possible . . . so, truly, anything is possible for *them*! This relationship can work long distance, as a fling, or something more long term, as long as both are willing to compromise and keep communication open (no mind games!). These two may argue when Pisces realizes that Sagittarius sees things in a more black-and-white way than they do. Sagittarius is sanctimonious in a way that Pisces has a hard time relating to.

Sagittarius's stamina is thrilling for Pisces, and Pisces's imagination keeps Sagittarius interested: both signs crave variety. If they choose to build a home together, it's sure to be filled with amazing scores from flea markets and antique stores, as well as plenty of books, maps, and guides. Pisces would be wise to show Sag how socially connected they are and to reveal their intellect and wit. Freedom-seeking Sag needs to prove to Pisces that they can be reliable, which they often are for those they love!

PISCES & CAPRICORN

Capricorn is dry and practical, but Pisces, the fish, is all wet and abstract. That's okay—in fact, these differences are just what pull these two together. Pisces is able to teach Capricorn new ways of looking at the world and remind them that things aren't always as plain as they seem—something these jaded sea goats need to be reminded of. Capricorn encourages Pisces to chase their dreams in a way that is responsible and organized, and Capricorn often knows just the right people to introduce Pisces to—Capricorn is usually well connected.

Capricorn is often seeking to be part of a power couple, and while Pisces doesn't really care about being in the VIP section, Capricorn will be proud to have such a creative person at their side. Often referred to as the workaholic of the zodiac, Capricorn does crave a warm home, so Pisces would be wise to tap into the homemaker in them if they want to seduce Capricorn.

Capricorn understands Pisces's sometimes dark sense of humor, and communication between these two is strong, making for a fun time in the bedroom, as they are able to talk about what turns them on—and off—easily. Pisces thinks Capricorn is one of the coolest people they've ever met; whether they meet Capricorn out with friends or online, they see them as someone who commands attention, who knows what's up, who has it under control—yet has a devilish sense of humor.

PISCES & AQUARIUS

Pisces is deeply empathetic, and as the old soul of the zodiac, there isn't much Pisces hasn't seen. But it's still hard for them to wrap their mind around Aquarius! What's life without some ambiguity? Pisces and Aquarius will bond over their common love of mysteries and the unknown.

Pisces can break the ice with this cool Air sign by chatting with them about horror movies, science fiction, conspiracy theories, and the paranormal. A mutual desire to explore the unknown will make for an interesting first encounter in the bedroom, as these two will be very excited to see what turns the other person on.

With Aquarius, Pisces thinks deeply about their own shadow side, unconscious behaviors, and deep-seated fears. Aquarius is the genius of the zodiac, and like Pisces, they are wildly creative; however, Pisces has an easier time tapping into the more artistic, poetic side of their creativity, which is something Aquarius deeply admires about them. Pisces shouldn't be shy to show off this quality.

Sometimes, when Pisces is shy, it confuses Aquarius into thinking they are bored or uninterested. These two may clash when discussing emotional issues because their communication styles are very different—Aquarius feels most comfortable talking in a very clinical fashion, using terms they pulled from a book about effective communication, which to Pisces may feel condescending. But they both have a deep need for freedom and don't care about fitting in with the crowd. This shared attitude about life will lead these two into being, at least, great friends, and at best, partners who are able to push each other forward in unexpected ways.

PISCES & PISCES

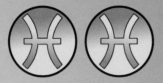

As the last sign in the zodiac, Pisces isn't always fantastic at "taking the lead," so when these fish meet they are likely to slowly swim circles around each other until the perfect moment arrives for them to come together romantically. This waiting can be extremely sexy—looks of longing across a smoky dance floor are excruciatingly stressful, leaving the fish to wonder whether they are cool, hot, or smart enough. Being, doing, creating *enough* is a fear the fish know well.

If the fish are able to eventually come together and begin a romance, they will find themselves with someone who matches them in empathy, creativity, and depth. But they may not be on the same page of maturity and experience around managing their psychic abilities, asserting their boundaries, or handling their paranoia. Pisces is prone to escapism, and if this couple can't find healthy ways to engage in this together, it could prove to be a problem.

However, if the fish are able to productively live in the real world together, and enjoy their dream world of love, they'll find a deep joy between them. These two fish will have finally met someone who can understand the deep lows and profound highs that they both experience.

A Pisces couple shares compatible life goals of seeing the world and expanding their minds, and sexually, they're both giving and eager to explore one another's fantasies. Their home is sure to be filled with books and movies, as these two love to consume media and discuss art. Their kitchen is likely stocked with all sorts of interesting tools, too—they may not know how to use them all, but they love entertaining (and nourishing) their friends.

Glossary

Air: One of the four elements, Air signs include Gemini, Libra, and Aquarius. They see the word through a logical lens and value communication. Even when they find themselves caught up in drama, they manage to be friends with everyone! They're big flirts who love to be partnered up.

Cardinal: Cardinal signs are the first signs of each season: Aries, Cancer, Libra, and Capricorn. They are leaders and initiators, so they're not afraid to make the first move or express interest.

Earth: One of the four elements, Earth signs include Taurus, Virgo, and Capricorn. They see the world through a material lens and are practical people. They can be grumpy, but they're hard workers, solid friends, and sensual lovers.

Fire: One of the four elements, Fire signs include Aries, Leo, and Sagittarius. They see the world through an inspired, passionate lens; these signs have plenty of willpower. They can be impatient and impulsive, but they know how to have fun, and they'll always have your back.

Fixed: Fixed signs are the middle signs of each season: Taurus, Leo, Scorpio, and Aquarius. Fixed signs are stable and determined. They call you back when they say they will.

Mutable: Mutable signs are the last signs of each season: Gemini, Virgo, Sagittarius, and Pisces. They are adaptable and communicative. Expect your conversations with these signs to go late into the evening.

Water: One of the four elements, Water signs include Cancer, Scorpio, and Pisces. They see the world through an emotional lens and are known for being intuitive. They can be moody crybabies, but they know how to love deeply and are tougher than they seem—never underestimate the depth and power of water!

Acknowledgments

Thank you so much to my supportive and loving family, especially my mom, and to my first astrology teachers, Anne Ortelee and Mark Wolz. There are so many friends, colleagues, mentors, and students who I have to thank for encouraging and supporting me, and giving me feedback on this book: Lucy Goldstein and Rachel Goldstein, Liza Mann, Heather Breen, Callie Beusman, Lindsay Schrupp, Sara David and the whole team at Broadly, Zita, Janx, Rutger, Niko, Cho, Mike and Q, Jardy Clemente, Wade Karshis, Jessica Lanyadoo, Ashley Otero, Barry Perlman, Priya Kale, Lisa Stardust, Randon Rosenbohm, Aliza Kelly Faragher, Danny Larkin, Emily Newhouse, Steph Koyfman, Lexi Ferguson, Liana Mack, Sophie Saint Thomas, Oriana Fine, Darla Downing, Arwen Falk, Elizabeth DeCoursey, Hilary Dare, Aerinn Kolfage, TC Eisele, Cat Cabral, Ammo O'Day, Jeanette Montesano, Hope Diamond, Lorry Kikta, Kristi Collom, Julie Tibbot, Zaneta Jung, and Chronicle Books.